Cloud Identity Management: the complete guide

James Relington

DEDICATION

To all cybersecurity professionals. Your commitment to protecting access, enforcing governance, and navigating the complexities of identity management is invaluable. May this work serve as a guide and inspiration in your ongoing efforts to create a more secure and compliant future.

AKNOWLEDGEMENTS

I extend my deepest gratitude to everyone who contributed to the creation of this book. To my colleagues and mentors in the field of identity governance, your insights and expertise have been invaluable. To my friends and family, your unwavering support and encouragement have made this journey possible. To the professionals and innovators dedicated to securing digital identities, your work continues to inspire and shape the future of cybersecurity. This book is a reflection of collective knowledge, and I am grateful to all who have played a role in its development.

Introduction to Cloud Identity Management

Cloud Identity Management has become an essential aspect of modern IT infrastructure, enabling organizations to securely manage user identities, control access to resources, and ensure compliance with security policies. As businesses continue migrating to cloud-based environments, traditional identity management methods have proven inadequate in handling the scale, flexibility, and security challenges associated with cloud computing. Cloud Identity Management solutions address these challenges by providing a centralized, scalable, and automated approach to user authentication, authorization, and governance.

At the core of Cloud Identity Management is the concept of identity as a service (IDaaS), which allows organizations to manage identities without maintaining on-premises infrastructure. IDaaS solutions provide authentication, single sign-on (SSO), multi-factor authentication (MFA), and access management functionalities through cloud-based platforms. These services help businesses reduce costs, enhance security, and streamline access control across various applications and services. By shifting identity management to the cloud, organizations can improve user experience, reduce the risk of credential theft, and gain better visibility into access patterns.

One of the key components of Cloud Identity Management is authentication, which ensures that only legitimate users can access systems and applications. Traditional authentication methods, such as passwords, are no longer sufficient due to the increasing sophistication of cyber threats. As a result, cloud identity providers incorporate advanced authentication mechanisms, including biometric authentication, adaptive authentication, and MFA, to enhance security. MFA, for example, requires users to provide multiple forms of verification, such as a password and a mobile push notification, before gaining access to critical resources.

Another crucial aspect of Cloud Identity Management is access control, which determines what users can do once they have been authenticated. Role-Based Access Control (RBAC) and Attribute-Based

Access Control (ABAC) are commonly used models to define access permissions. RBAC assigns roles to users based on their job functions, ensuring that they only have access to the information necessary for their responsibilities. ABAC, on the other hand, considers attributes such as device type, location, and time of access to enforce more dynamic access policies. These access control models help organizations minimize the risk of unauthorized data exposure and prevent privilege escalation attacks.

Cloud Identity Management also enables seamless integration with various cloud applications and services. As businesses adopt Software-as-a-Service (SaaS) applications, managing user access across multiple platforms can become complex. Cloud identity providers address this challenge by offering identity federation, which allows users to authenticate once and access multiple applications without needing to log in separately. Standards such as Security Assertion Markup Language (SAML), OpenID Connect, and OAuth enable secure authentication and authorization across different systems, improving both security and user convenience.

Another advantage of Cloud Identity Management is its ability to provide identity governance and compliance capabilities. Organizations must comply with regulatory requirements such as GDPR, HIPAA, and SOC 2, which mandate strict access control, audit logging, and data protection measures. Cloud Identity Management solutions offer automated user provisioning and de-provisioning, ensuring that employees, contractors, and partners have the right level of access at the right time. Additionally, audit logs and reporting functionalities help security teams monitor access activities, detect anomalies, and demonstrate compliance during audits.

As cyber threats continue to evolve, organizations must adopt a Zero Trust approach to identity management. Zero Trust is a security model that assumes no user or device should be inherently trusted, requiring continuous verification before granting access. Cloud Identity Management solutions support Zero Trust principles by enforcing strict authentication policies, continuously monitoring user behavior, and leveraging risk-based access controls. By implementing a Zero Trust strategy, businesses can reduce the risk of insider threats, credential theft, and lateral movement attacks.

Cloud Identity Management also plays a critical role in supporting remote work and hybrid workforce models. With employees accessing corporate resources from various locations and devices, organizations must ensure secure and frictionless authentication experiences. Identity providers offer solutions such as adaptive authentication, conditional access policies, and endpoint security integrations to enable secure remote access while maintaining a seamless user experience. These capabilities allow businesses to support a distributed workforce without compromising security.

Furthermore, Cloud Identity Management enhances operational efficiency by automating identity lifecycle management. Traditional identity management processes often involve manual user provisioning, password resets, and access reviews, leading to inefficiencies and security gaps. Cloud-based identity solutions automate these processes by integrating with HR systems, IT service management platforms, and security tools. Automated user provisioning ensures that new employees receive the appropriate access on their first day, while automated de-provisioning promptly revokes access when employees leave the organization. These automation capabilities reduce administrative overhead, enhance security, and improve compliance.

As organizations continue their digital transformation journeys, the role of Cloud Identity Management will become even more significant. Emerging technologies such as artificial intelligence (AI) and machine learning (ML) are being integrated into identity management solutions to enhance threat detection, automate risk assessments, and improve user authentication experiences. AI-powered identity analytics can identify abnormal login patterns, detect compromised credentials, and trigger real-time security responses. These innovations will further strengthen the security posture of businesses while minimizing user friction.

Cloud Identity Management is no longer a luxury but a necessity for organizations operating in today's digital landscape. As cyber threats grow in sophistication and businesses expand their cloud adoption, having a robust identity management strategy is crucial. By leveraging cloud-based identity solutions, organizations can enhance security, improve operational efficiency, and ensure compliance with regulatory requirements. The future of identity management will continue to evolve, driven by advancements in authentication technologies, AI-driven security insights, and Zero Trust security models. Organizations that prioritize Cloud Identity Management will be better positioned to safeguard their digital assets and support their workforce in an increasingly interconnected world.

Understanding the Identity Lifecycle

Identity management is a critical component of modern digital infrastructure, ensuring that users, devices, and systems have appropriate access to resources while maintaining security and compliance. The identity lifecycle represents the entire process of managing user identities from creation to retirement, encompassing key stages such as provisioning, authentication, role management, auditing, and deprovisioning. As organizations move toward cloud-based identity solutions, understanding the identity lifecycle becomes essential for ensuring security, efficiency, and regulatory compliance.

The first stage of the identity lifecycle is identity creation and provisioning. When a new employee, contractor, or system account is introduced to an organization, an identity must be created within the relevant identity management system. This includes assigning a unique identifier, credentials, and initial access permissions based on predefined policies. Provisioning may involve integrating multiple identity stores, such as Active Directory, cloud-based identity providers, or federated authentication systems. Automation plays a key role in this phase, enabling rapid user onboarding while reducing the risk of errors and security vulnerabilities.

Once an identity is provisioned, it moves into the authentication and access management phase. Authentication ensures that users are who they claim to be, using mechanisms such as passwords, multi-factor authentication (MFA), or biometric verification. This phase also involves single sign-on (SSO) solutions that allow users to access multiple applications with a single set of credentials, improving both security and user experience. Access management, on the other hand, ensures that users only have the necessary permissions required to perform their tasks. Organizations often implement role-based access control (RBAC) or attribute-based access control (ABAC) to manage user access dynamically based on job roles, departments, or risk factors.

As identities continue to be used within an organization, they must be actively managed and monitored. This includes periodic access reviews to ensure that users still require their assigned permissions. Over time, employees may change roles, take on new responsibilities, or switch departments, necessitating updates to their identity attributes and access rights. Without proper governance, access creep can occur, where users accumulate unnecessary permissions over time, increasing the risk of security breaches. To mitigate this, organizations implement identity governance frameworks that enforce policies for access certification, least privilege, and separation of duties.

Another critical aspect of the identity lifecycle is compliance and auditing. Regulatory frameworks such as GDPR, HIPAA, and SOC 2 require organizations to maintain detailed records of identity and access management activities. Identity auditing ensures that access logs, authentication events, and privilege escalations are continuously monitored for anomalies. Organizations utilize security information and event management (SIEM) tools to analyze identity-related events and detect potential security incidents. This proactive approach helps in identifying unauthorized access attempts, compromised accounts, and policy violations before they can escalate into larger security threats.

Eventually, every identity must reach the deprovisioning stage. When an employee leaves an organization, a contractor's contract ends, or a system account is no longer needed, the associated identity must be deactivated and removed from all systems. Deprovisioning ensures that access is revoked in a timely manner, reducing the risk of orphaned accounts that could be exploited by malicious actors. Automated deprovisioning processes help organizations enforce policies for account termination, including disabling accounts, revoking credentials, and removing access to cloud services and on-premises applications. Proper deprovisioning practices also include data retention policies, ensuring that any residual user data is handled according to regulatory and business requirements.

Throughout the identity lifecycle, automation and artificial intelligence (AI) are transforming how organizations manage identities. AI-driven identity analytics enable real-time risk assessments, anomaly detection, and behavior-based authentication adjustments. Machine learning algorithms help identify patterns of suspicious activity, such as sudden changes in user behavior or login attempts from unusual locations. Additionally, AI-powered automation streamlines identity provisioning, access requests, and compliance enforcement, reducing administrative overhead while improving security posture.

Cloud identity management has introduced new challenges and opportunities in the identity lifecycle. Unlike traditional on-premises identity solutions, cloud-based identity platforms provide scalability, agility, and integration with diverse applications and services. However, managing identities in a multi-cloud environment requires federated identity strategies, API-driven identity synchronization, and zero-trust security models. Organizations must ensure that identity lifecycle processes align with their broader cloud security strategy, implementing policies that adapt to dynamic workloads and distributed user populations.

Effective identity lifecycle management also enhances the overall user experience. Employees benefit from seamless onboarding processes, self-service password resets, and automated access approvals, allowing them to focus on productivity rather than administrative hurdles. At the same time, IT and security teams gain better visibility into identity-related risks, enabling them to enforce security policies without impeding business operations. By striking a balance between security, usability, and compliance, organizations can create a robust identity management framework that supports both operational efficiency and cybersecurity resilience.

Ultimately, identity lifecycle management is not a static process but an evolving discipline that must adapt to technological advancements, regulatory changes, and emerging security threats. Organizations that implement strong identity governance, automation, and continuous monitoring will be better positioned to protect sensitive data, reduce identity-related risks, and ensure seamless access to resources for their users. Managing the identity lifecycle effectively is a cornerstone of modern security and operational strategy, helping organizations navigate the complexities of digital transformation while maintaining trust and compliance.

Identity Federation in Cloud Environments

Identity federation in cloud environments is a crucial aspect of modern digital identity management. As organizations increasingly adopt cloud services, managing user identities across multiple platforms becomes complex. Identity federation provides a seamless and secure way to enable users to access multiple systems using a single identity. This reduces the burden of maintaining multiple credentials and enhances security by minimizing attack surfaces. By enabling trust between identity providers and service providers, organizations can streamline authentication processes, improve user experience, and maintain strong security postures.

At the heart of identity federation is the concept of trust between different organizations or systems. A user's identity is verified by an identity provider (IdP), which then asserts this identity to a service provider (SP). The SP relies on the authentication performed by the IdP, eliminating the need for separate user accounts and passwords across different applications. This approach is particularly beneficial in hybrid cloud environments, where users need to access on-premises and cloud-based services seamlessly.

Federated identity management relies on standards such as Security Assertion Markup Language (SAML), Open Authorization (OAuth), and OpenID Connect. These protocols facilitate secure communication between IdPs and SPs, ensuring that authentication data is exchanged in a standardized and secure manner. SAML, for example, allows identity assertions to be transmitted via XML-based messages, while OAuth provides delegated access without exposing user credentials. OpenID Connect, an extension of OAuth, enables authentication and single sign-on (SSO) capabilities, further enhancing usability and security.

One of the key advantages of identity federation is reducing password fatigue. Users no longer need to remember multiple usernames and passwords for different services. Instead, they authenticate once with the IdP, and their credentials are securely shared with trusted SPs. This not only improves the user experience but also mitigates security risks associated with weak or reused passwords. Additionally, organizations can enforce strong authentication policies at the IdP level, such as requiring multi-factor authentication (MFA), further strengthening security.

Another significant benefit is centralized access control and policy enforcement. By managing identities at the IdP level, organizations can define access policies that apply across multiple applications and services. This simplifies compliance with security regulations and ensures that users only have access to the resources they need based on predefined roles and permissions. In industries with strict regulatory requirements, such as finance and healthcare, identity federation helps maintain audit trails and access logs, facilitating compliance reporting.

Cloud-based identity federation is also essential for enabling secure collaboration between organizations. Businesses often need to provide access to external partners, contractors, or customers without creating separate accounts for them in internal directories. By establishing trust relationships between different IdPs, organizations can grant controlled access to external users while maintaining security and governance. This is particularly useful in supply chain management, where multiple entities must interact securely without exposing internal systems.

Despite its advantages, implementing identity federation comes with challenges. Organizations must establish trust relationships between different IdPs and SPs, which requires careful planning and configuration. Additionally, interoperability between different identity providers and cloud platforms can be complex, requiring adherence to standardized protocols and best practices. Security considerations, such as protecting identity tokens and preventing unauthorized access, must also be addressed through robust encryption and monitoring mechanisms.

Performance and scalability are also important factors in identity federation. As user volumes increase, authentication requests must be processed efficiently without causing delays. Organizations need to optimize their IdP infrastructure, use load balancing techniques, and ensure redundancy to maintain availability. Cloud identity solutions often provide scalability features, but proper configuration and continuous monitoring are necessary to avoid performance bottlenecks.

As organizations continue their digital transformation journeys, identity federation will play an increasingly vital role in securing cloud environments. By leveraging federated identity management, businesses can simplify authentication processes, enhance security, and improve user experience across cloud-based applications and services. While challenges exist, adopting best practices, following security standards, and leveraging modern identity management solutions can help organizations successfully implement identity federation in their cloud ecosystems.

Role-Based Access Control in Practice

Role-Based Access Control (RBAC) is one of the most widely implemented access control models in modern identity management. It is designed to ensure that users only have access to the resources necessary for their job functions while preventing unauthorized access to sensitive data and systems. By assigning roles to users based on their responsibilities, organizations can enforce security policies more effectively, reduce administrative overhead, and minimize the risks associated with excessive permissions. Implementing RBAC in practice requires careful planning, integration with existing identity and access management (IAM) systems, and continuous monitoring to adapt to organizational changes.

At its core, RBAC revolves around the concept of defining roles within an organization and associating those roles with specific permissions. Each role represents a set of privileges that correspond to tasks or responsibilities performed by employees, contractors, or system accounts. For example, a financial analyst in a company may have access to financial reporting tools and accounting databases, while a software developer might be granted permissions to source code repositories and development environments. By structuring access in this way, organizations can simplify permission management and enhance security by enforcing the principle of least privilege.

One of the primary benefits of RBAC is its ability to streamline user provisioning and deprovisioning. When a new employee joins an organization, they can be assigned a predefined role based on their department, job function, or seniority level. This eliminates the need for administrators to manually configure access permissions for each individual user, reducing the risk of errors and inconsistencies. Similarly, when an employee leaves the company or transitions to a different role, their previous permissions can be revoked or adjusted automatically, ensuring that access remains aligned with their current responsibilities.

Implementing RBAC in an enterprise environment requires a thorough analysis of business processes, role definitions, and access requirements. The first step is to conduct a role discovery process, where IT and security teams work closely with department leaders to identify the various job functions within the organization. This involves cataloging existing permissions, mapping them to job responsibilities, and grouping them into logical roles. While this process can be complex, it is essential for ensuring that roles accurately reflect operational needs without granting excessive or unnecessary privileges.

Once roles have been defined, they must be implemented within the organization's IAM system. Many modern IAM platforms, including cloud-based identity providers, offer built-in support for RBAC. Administrators can create roles, assign users to those roles, and enforce access policies through centralized management consoles. Additionally, role hierarchies can be established to reflect organizational structures, where higher-level roles inherit permissions from lower-level roles. For example, a senior manager may have all the permissions of a standard employee, along with additional privileges related to approving transactions or accessing confidential reports.

RBAC can also be combined with other access control models to enhance security and flexibility. Attribute-Based Access Control (ABAC), for instance, extends RBAC by incorporating dynamic attributes such as time of access, device type, or geographic location. This allows organizations to enforce more granular access policies that adapt to real-world scenarios. For example, a role assigned to a financial analyst may grant access to sensitive reports only during business hours and only from corporate-issued devices. By integrating RBAC with contextual factors, organizations can strengthen security while maintaining operational efficiency.

One of the challenges in implementing RBAC is role explosion, where the number of roles becomes unmanageable due to overly specific definitions. Organizations must strike a balance between granularity and simplicity to avoid excessive administrative overhead. Role mining and automation tools can help analyze existing permissions, detect redundant roles, and optimize role structures to ensure efficiency. Additionally, periodic role reviews should be conducted to ensure that assigned roles remain relevant and that users do not accumulate unnecessary privileges over time.

RBAC also plays a critical role in compliance and audit requirements. Regulations such as GDPR, HIPAA, and SOX mandate strict access controls and audit trails to protect sensitive data. By enforcing RBAC policies, organizations can demonstrate compliance by ensuring that access is granted based on defined roles rather than arbitrary decisions. Audit logs can provide a clear record of access requests, role assignments, and permission changes, allowing security teams to identify potential policy violations and mitigate insider threats.

In cloud environments, RBAC is essential for securing access to cloud applications, infrastructure, and services. Cloud providers such as AWS, Microsoft Azure, and Google Cloud offer RBAC-based access control mechanisms that allow organizations to define roles for administrators, developers, and operations teams. These roles determine who can manage virtual machines, configure network settings, or deploy applications. By implementing RBAC across cloud environments, organizations can enforce consistent security policies while maintaining agility in cloud operations.

Adopting RBAC is not a one-time implementation but an ongoing process that requires continuous monitoring, role adjustments, and policy enforcement. As organizations evolve, new roles may be introduced, existing roles may become obsolete, and security threats may necessitate stricter access controls. Automation tools and identity analytics can help organizations proactively manage roles, detect anomalies, and refine access policies to align with business objectives.

RBAC is a foundational element of modern identity management, enabling organizations to enforce structured access controls, enhance security, and streamline administrative processes. By defining clear roles, integrating RBAC with IAM solutions, and continuously optimizing access policies, organizations can create a secure and efficient access control framework. The successful implementation of RBAC requires collaboration between IT, security, and business teams to ensure that access permissions align with operational needs while mitigating risks. As threats evolve and technology advances, RBAC will continue to play a vital role in securing digital assets and supporting compliance requirements.

Multi-Factor Authentication Strategies

Multi-Factor Authentication (MFA) has become a fundamental security measure for protecting user identities and preventing unauthorized access to digital systems. As cyber threats evolve, relying solely on passwords is no longer sufficient to ensure security. MFA enhances authentication by requiring users to provide multiple forms of verification before accessing a system, reducing the likelihood of account compromise. Organizations across industries are implementing MFA strategies to protect sensitive data, mitigate credential-based attacks, and meet regulatory requirements.

MFA operates on the principle of requiring at least two out of three authentication factors: something the user knows (such as a password or PIN), something the user has (such as a security token or mobile device), and something the user is (such as biometric data like fingerprints or facial recognition). By combining multiple factors, MFA makes it significantly more difficult for attackers to gain unauthorized access, even if one factor is compromised. For example, if a user's password is stolen in a phishing attack, an additional factor—such as a time-sensitive authentication code sent to their phone—can prevent the attacker from accessing the account.

One of the most commonly used MFA strategies is SMS-based authentication, where users receive a one-time passcode (OTP) via text message. While this method is easy to deploy and widely adopted, it has vulnerabilities. Attackers can intercept SMS messages through SIM-swapping attacks or network exploits, making this method less secure than other MFA options. Despite its weaknesses, SMS-based MFA still provides a higher level of security than password-only authentication and remains a viable option for organizations that need a simple implementation.

A more secure alternative is app-based authentication, which relies on mobile applications such as Google Authenticator, Microsoft Authenticator, or Authy. These apps generate time-based one-time passwords (TOTP) that expire after a short duration, reducing the risk of interception. Since the codes are generated locally on the user's device rather than transmitted over a network, this method is considered more secure than SMS-based authentication. Many organizations encourage users to switch from SMS to app-based authentication for improved security.

Hardware tokens offer another layer of protection, especially in high-security environments. Devices such as YubiKeys or RSA SecurID tokens generate cryptographic authentication codes that users must enter to verify their identity. Some hardware tokens also support Universal 2nd Factor (U2F) authentication, allowing users to authenticate by simply tapping the device when prompted. These physical security keys are highly resistant to phishing attacks and are widely used in industries that require strong authentication mechanisms, such as finance and government.

Biometric authentication is an increasingly popular MFA strategy that leverages unique physical characteristics for identity verification. Fingerprint recognition, facial recognition, and iris scanning are among the most commonly used biometric methods. Modern smartphones and laptops often include built-in biometric sensors, making this form of authentication both secure and convenient. Biometric authentication is difficult to replicate, adding a strong layer of security. However, privacy concerns and the risk of biometric data leaks must be addressed through proper encryption and storage mechanisms.

Adaptive authentication, also known as risk-based authentication, enhances MFA by dynamically adjusting authentication requirements based on contextual factors. This approach analyzes elements such as the user's location, device, behavior patterns, and login history to determine the level of risk. If a login attempt is deemed low-risk—such as a user accessing their account from a trusted device in a familiar location—MFA challenges may be minimized. Conversely, if an attempt originates from an unfamiliar device or location, additional authentication steps may be triggered. Adaptive authentication balances security with user convenience by reducing unnecessary friction while maintaining robust protection against threats.

Push-based authentication is another MFA strategy that improves both security and user experience. Instead of requiring users to enter a code, push authentication sends a real-time notification to their mobile device, asking them to approve or deny the login attempt. This method is widely used by services such as Duo Security and Okta Verify. Push authentication is highly resistant to phishing attacks since the user must actively confirm the login request, making it more difficult for attackers to gain access.

Organizations implementing MFA must also consider usability and user adoption. While MFA significantly enhances security, poorly designed authentication processes can frustrate users and lead to resistance. To ensure a smooth implementation, businesses should provide clear guidance, user-friendly authentication methods, and fallback options for account recovery. Educating employees and customers about the importance of MFA can also increase adoption rates and reduce instances of users bypassing security measures.

Compliance with regulatory standards is another driving force behind MFA adoption. Many regulations, such as the General Data Protection Regulation (GDPR), the Payment Card Industry Data Security Standard (PCI DSS), and the Cybersecurity Maturity Model

Certification (CMMC), mandate strong authentication controls to protect sensitive data. Organizations that fail to implement MFA may face financial penalties, legal consequences, or reputational damage. By deploying MFA solutions, businesses can demonstrate compliance while strengthening their overall security posture.

While MFA significantly enhances security, it is not foolproof. Cybercriminals continuously develop sophisticated attack techniques, such as man-in-the-middle (MITM) attacks and MFA fatigue attacks, where repeated push notifications are sent to trick users into approving fraudulent login attempts. To counter these threats, organizations should combine MFA with other security measures, such as endpoint protection, network monitoring, and user behavior analytics. Implementing phishing-resistant authentication methods, such as FIDO2-compliant security keys, can further reduce the risk of account compromise.

As technology continues to evolve, the future of MFA will likely involve passwordless authentication methods that rely solely on biometrics, cryptographic keys, or decentralized identity solutions. Advances in artificial intelligence (AI) and machine learning will also enhance adaptive authentication, making MFA more intelligent and responsive to emerging threats. Organizations that stay ahead of these trends and continuously improve their authentication strategies will be better equipped to protect their digital assets in an increasingly complex cybersecurity landscape.

Single Sign-On (SSO) and Its Benefits

Single Sign-On (SSO) is a fundamental identity management solution that simplifies authentication across multiple applications and services. In an era where organizations rely on various cloud-based and on-premises systems, managing user credentials separately for each platform is inefficient and introduces security risks. SSO addresses these challenges by allowing users to authenticate once and gain access to multiple resources without needing to re-enter credentials. This enhances security, improves user experience, and reduces the administrative burden associated with password management.

At the core of SSO is the concept of centralized authentication. Instead of requiring users to maintain multiple usernames and passwords, SSO enables them to authenticate through a single identity provider (IdP). Once the user successfully logs in, authentication tokens or session credentials are issued and used to access connected applications. This approach eliminates the need for repetitive logins and ensures that authentication policies are consistently applied across all services. Organizations can integrate SSO with their existing directory services, identity providers, and authentication mechanisms to create a seamless access experience for employees, partners, and customers.

Security Assertion Markup Language (SAML), OpenID Connect, and OAuth are widely used protocols that facilitate SSO implementations. SAML, an XML-based standard, allows identity providers to authenticate users and pass secure assertions to service providers. OpenID Connect, built on top of OAuth, enables authentication and authorization through modern web-based APIs. These protocols ensure that authentication data is securely exchanged between systems, reducing the risk of credential exposure. By leveraging standardized authentication mechanisms, organizations can ensure interoperability between different identity providers and cloud applications.

One of the primary benefits of SSO is the reduction of password fatigue. Users often struggle with managing multiple passwords for various systems, leading to poor security practices such as reusing passwords or writing them down. SSO mitigates this issue by requiring users to remember only a single set of credentials. This not only enhances security but also improves productivity, as employees spend less time recovering lost passwords or dealing with account lockouts. By implementing SSO, organizations can enforce strong password policies while reducing the likelihood of weak or compromised passwords being used across multiple services.

Another advantage of SSO is its ability to strengthen security through centralized authentication controls. By consolidating authentication through a trusted identity provider, organizations can enforce multi-factor authentication (MFA), risk-based authentication, and adaptive access policies. For example, if a user attempts to log in from an unrecognized device or unusual location, the system can prompt for additional verification before granting access. These security measures help prevent unauthorized access while maintaining a seamless login experience for legitimate users.

SSO also plays a crucial role in improving user experience. In large organizations, employees often need to access numerous applications daily, from email and collaboration tools to customer relationship management (CRM) and enterprise resource planning (ERP) systems. Without SSO, users would have to log in separately to each system, leading to frustration and decreased efficiency. With SSO, users authenticate once and gain access to all authorized applications, creating a more streamlined and productive workflow. This benefit extends beyond employees to external partners, vendors, and customers who interact with multiple systems within an organization's ecosystem.

From an administrative perspective, SSO significantly reduces IT workload and operational costs. Help desks spend a substantial amount of time handling password-related issues, such as resets and account unlocks. By reducing the number of credentials users must manage, SSO lowers the volume of password reset requests and decreases IT support costs. Additionally, centralized authentication simplifies user provisioning and deprovisioning, ensuring that access is granted or revoked efficiently based on role changes, employment status, or security policies.

Compliance and regulatory requirements further highlight the importance of SSO. Organizations operating in regulated industries, such as healthcare, finance, and government, must adhere to strict security and privacy standards. Regulations like GDPR, HIPAA, and SOC 2 mandate secure access controls, audit trails, and data protection measures. SSO helps organizations achieve compliance by providing centralized logging and monitoring capabilities, enabling security teams to track authentication events, detect anomalies, and generate compliance reports. By implementing SSO, businesses can demonstrate adherence to regulatory requirements while minimizing security risks.

Despite its numerous advantages, implementing SSO requires careful planning and execution. Organizations must select the right identity provider and authentication protocols to align with their security and business needs. Integration with existing identity and access management (IAM) systems, cloud services, and legacy applications can present challenges that require technical expertise. Additionally, ensuring high availability and resilience is critical, as a failure in the SSO infrastructure could disrupt access to multiple systems. Organizations must implement redundancy, failover mechanisms, and robust security controls to mitigate potential risks.

Modern SSO solutions are evolving to support hybrid and multi-cloud environments. As businesses adopt SaaS applications, cloud infrastructure, and remote work models, identity management becomes more complex. Cloud-based SSO platforms provide scalability and flexibility, allowing organizations to extend secure authentication across various cloud services and on-premises applications. Additionally, advancements in artificial intelligence (AI) and machine learning (ML) are enhancing SSO capabilities, enabling intelligent authentication, anomaly detection, and real-time risk analysis.

SSO is a cornerstone of modern identity management, offering significant benefits in terms of security, user experience, and administrative efficiency. By enabling seamless authentication across multiple applications, reducing password-related vulnerabilities, and providing centralized security controls, SSO enhances overall security posture while simplifying access management. Organizations that implement SSO effectively can improve productivity, strengthen compliance, and reduce operational costs. As identity management continues to evolve, SSO will remain a key enabler of secure and efficient digital access in cloud-driven environments.

Identity Governance Fundamentals

Identity governance is a critical component of modern security frameworks, ensuring that organizations effectively manage digital identities, enforce compliance policies, and minimize security risks. As businesses continue expanding their use of cloud services and remote work environments, maintaining control over user access has become increasingly complex. Identity governance provides the necessary tools and processes to oversee identity lifecycle management, access controls, and compliance auditing while reducing the risk of unauthorized access and data breaches.

At the core of identity governance is the principle of visibility and control over user identities and their access rights. Organizations must establish clear policies for managing identities across various systems, applications, and cloud platforms. Without governance mechanisms in place, users may accumulate excessive permissions over time, leading to security vulnerabilities. By implementing strict access control policies, organizations can ensure that employees, contractors, and third parties only have the permissions required for their specific roles.

Identity governance involves defining and enforcing policies related to user provisioning, role-based access control (RBAC), and attribute-based access control (ABAC). User provisioning ensures that employees receive appropriate access when they join an organization and that their permissions are updated or revoked as their roles change. Automated provisioning processes help maintain efficiency while reducing the likelihood of human error. Role-based access control assigns permissions based on predefined job roles, simplifying access management, while attribute-based access control provides more granular access control by incorporating contextual factors such as location, device type, and time of access.

One of the primary objectives of identity governance is to prevent unauthorized access and mitigate the risk of insider threats. Organizations must implement periodic access reviews to validate whether users still require their assigned permissions. Access certification processes enable managers and security teams to verify that users have appropriate access levels, reducing the risk of privilege creep. When employees change roles, departments, or leave the organization, their previous access rights must be revoked promptly to prevent potential security gaps.

Identity governance also plays a crucial role in regulatory compliance. Various industries are subject to strict regulations such as GDPR, HIPAA, SOX, and PCI DSS, which require organizations to maintain detailed records of user access and enforce security best practices.

Governance tools facilitate compliance by automating access reviews, generating audit reports, and providing real-time visibility into user activities. Organizations that fail to implement robust identity governance frameworks may face financial penalties, reputational damage, and legal consequences due to non-compliance.

The enforcement of least privilege access is a fundamental principle within identity governance. Users should only be granted the minimum level of access necessary to perform their job functions. This reduces the attack surface and limits the potential damage caused by compromised credentials or insider threats. Organizations can enforce least privilege policies by implementing just-in-time (JIT) access, where users are granted temporary access to resources based on specific needs rather than permanent privileges.

Identity governance solutions integrate with security information and event management (SIEM) systems to detect anomalies and potential security incidents. By analyzing login patterns, access requests, and privilege escalations, organizations can identify suspicious activities that may indicate account compromise or insider threats. Machine learning and artificial intelligence (AI) technologies further enhance governance by detecting unusual behavior and flagging potential risks in real time.

Another essential aspect of identity governance is privileged access management (PAM). Administrative and high-level accounts pose a significant security risk if not properly managed. Governance frameworks help organizations implement strict controls over privileged accounts, ensuring that only authorized personnel can access critical systems. Privileged session monitoring, password vaulting, and automated access approvals are some of the strategies used to secure privileged accounts and prevent misuse.

Organizations must also address identity governance challenges related to cloud environments and third-party access. With the adoption of multi-cloud and hybrid IT infrastructures, managing identities across different platforms becomes more complex. Cloud-based identity governance solutions offer centralized visibility and policy enforcement, allowing organizations to maintain control over cloud identities and external users. Third-party vendors and contractors should be subject to the same governance policies as internal employees, with automated onboarding and offboarding processes to prevent lingering access.

The implementation of identity governance requires a balance between security and user experience. While strict access controls and policies enhance security, they should not hinder productivity. Organizations must ensure that identity governance frameworks are designed to provide seamless user access while maintaining compliance and risk management. Self-service capabilities, automated access requests, and intelligent role recommendations can improve efficiency while reducing administrative overhead.

Identity governance is an ongoing process that evolves with an organization's security needs, regulatory landscape, and technological advancements. Continuous monitoring, policy adjustments, and user education are essential to maintaining an effective governance strategy. As cyber threats become more sophisticated, organizations must adapt their identity governance practices to address emerging risks and protect sensitive data from unauthorized access.

By adopting a comprehensive identity governance framework, organizations can strengthen security, streamline compliance efforts, and gain better visibility into user access. The integration of automation, AI-driven analytics, and adaptive access controls will further enhance governance capabilities, ensuring that identities are managed efficiently and securely across the enterprise. Organizations that prioritize identity governance will be better positioned to mitigate security risks, prevent unauthorized access, and maintain compliance in an increasingly complex digital environment.

Identity Synchronization Across Platforms

Identity synchronization across platforms is a critical component of modern identity management, ensuring seamless and secure access to resources across multiple systems. Organizations today operate in complex IT environments that include on-premises systems, cloud services, and hybrid infrastructures. Without effective identity synchronization, users may experience inconsistent access, security gaps, and administrative inefficiencies. Implementing a robust identity synchronization strategy allows businesses to maintain a unified identity framework, reduce duplication, and enhance security across platforms.

Identity synchronization refers to the process of maintaining consistency in user identities, attributes, and access permissions across different identity providers, directories, and applications. This ensures that changes made in one system—such as a password reset, role assignment, or account deactivation—are automatically reflected across all connected platforms. Without proper synchronization, organizations risk outdated credentials, orphaned accounts, and increased vulnerability to security threats.

One of the primary challenges of identity synchronization is integrating multiple identity sources. Many organizations rely on a combination of Active Directory (AD), Azure AD, LDAP directories, and cloud-based identity providers such as Okta, Google Workspace, and AWS IAM. Each of these systems may have different schemas, authentication mechanisms, and synchronization protocols. To address this complexity, organizations use identity synchronization tools and middleware to facilitate data consistency across platforms. These tools help bridge the gap between legacy and modern identity systems, ensuring users can authenticate seamlessly across all environments.

Federated identity management plays a crucial role in identity synchronization by allowing users to authenticate with a single set of credentials across multiple services. Standards such as Security Assertion Markup Language (SAML), OAuth, and OpenID Connect enable identity federation by establishing trust between identity providers and service providers. By leveraging federation, organizations can streamline authentication while maintaining centralized control over user identities. This approach reduces password fatigue, enhances security, and simplifies user provisioning and deprovisioning across platforms.

Automated provisioning and deprovisioning are essential aspects of identity synchronization. When a new employee joins an organization, their identity must be provisioned across all relevant applications, including email, collaboration tools, and enterprise resource planning (ERP) systems. Similarly, when an employee leaves or changes roles, their access permissions must be updated or revoked immediately to prevent unauthorized access. Identity synchronization ensures that these changes propagate in real-time, reducing administrative overhead and mitigating security risks.

Security and compliance considerations are integral to identity synchronization. Organizations must ensure that synchronized identity data remains protected against unauthorized access, data breaches, and compliance violations. Implementing encryption, secure APIs, and role-based access control (RBAC) helps safeguard identity synchronization processes. Additionally, audit logs and monitoring mechanisms should be in place to track synchronization activities and detect anomalies that may indicate security threats.

Cloud identity synchronization introduces additional complexities due to the dynamic nature of cloud services and multi-cloud environments. Many enterprises adopt hybrid identity solutions, where on-premises directories synchronize with cloud identity providers. Tools such as Azure AD Connect, Google Cloud Directory Sync, and AWS IAM Identity Center help organizations manage identity synchronization across diverse ecosystems. These solutions enable real-time updates, ensuring that user identities remain consistent regardless of where authentication occurs.

Another important aspect of identity synchronization is managing conflicts and inconsistencies. In large organizations with multiple identity sources, discrepancies in user attributes, duplicate accounts, or mismatched access rights can create operational challenges. Implementing identity resolution mechanisms, attribute mapping, and reconciliation processes helps resolve conflicts and maintain data integrity. Organizations should define clear synchronization policies, specifying how identity attributes are merged, prioritized, or overridden when discrepancies arise.

Identity synchronization also plays a crucial role in enabling Zero Trust security frameworks. Zero Trust principles require continuous verification of user identities, ensuring that access decisions are based on real-time risk assessments. By synchronizing identity attributes, authentication logs, and risk signals across platforms, organizations can enforce adaptive security policies. This approach strengthens access control mechanisms and reduces exposure to identity-based threats such as credential theft and account takeovers.

As identity synchronization technologies evolve, artificial intelligence (AI) and machine learning (ML) are being integrated into identity management systems to improve automation and threat detection. AI-powered identity analytics can identify unusual access patterns, detect synchronization anomalies, and automate identity lifecycle management tasks. These innovations enhance the efficiency and security of identity synchronization while reducing manual intervention and administrative overhead.

Effective identity synchronization requires a combination of strategic planning, advanced technologies, and continuous monitoring. Organizations must choose synchronization solutions that align with their security requirements, compliance obligations, and operational needs. By implementing standardized protocols, automation tools, and real-time monitoring, businesses can ensure seamless identity synchronization across platforms, enabling secure and efficient access for users while reducing the risk of security incidents.

Managing Identity Data Integrity

Managing identity data integrity is a critical aspect of modern cybersecurity and identity governance. Organizations rely on accurate, consistent, and secure identity data to authenticate users, enforce access controls, and comply with regulatory requirements. As enterprises expand their digital infrastructure across multiple platforms and cloud environments, maintaining identity data integrity becomes increasingly complex. Without proper data integrity measures, identity records can become inconsistent, leading to security vulnerabilities, compliance risks, and operational inefficiencies.

Identity data integrity refers to the accuracy, consistency, and reliability of user identity attributes across various identity systems. These attributes include usernames, email addresses, roles, access permissions, and authentication credentials. Ensuring that identity data remains accurate and synchronized across all systems is essential for preventing unauthorized access, mitigating insider threats, and enabling seamless user experiences. Identity data corruption, duplication, or mismanagement can lead to serious security breaches and compliance violations.

One of the key challenges in managing identity data integrity is data fragmentation. Organizations often store identity data in multiple directories, databases, and cloud platforms, leading to inconsistencies between different identity stores. When user attributes are not synchronized properly, outdated credentials, orphaned accounts, and conflicting access permissions can emerge. These inconsistencies can create security loopholes that attackers can exploit. To mitigate these risks, organizations must implement identity synchronization tools that ensure real-time updates across all platforms.

Data validation and normalization play an essential role in maintaining identity integrity. Identity data must be consistently formatted, verified, and standardized to prevent errors. For example, variations in how usernames or email addresses are stored across different systems can lead to duplicate accounts or authentication failures. Implementing automated validation processes helps ensure that identity attributes are correctly structured and meet predefined standards. Organizations should enforce policies that validate input data, detect anomalies, and flag inconsistencies before they create security risks.

Identity lifecycle management is another critical component of maintaining data integrity. Every user identity follows a lifecycle, from creation and provisioning to modification and deprovisioning. Organizations must ensure that changes to user roles, employment status, or access rights are reflected across all systems in a timely manner. Failure to properly manage identity lifecycles can result in outdated access permissions, allowing former employees or contractors to retain access to critical resources. Automating provisioning and deprovisioning workflows helps ensure that identity data remains accurate and up to date.

Auditing and monitoring identity data integrity are essential for detecting and addressing inconsistencies. Organizations should implement identity analytics and logging mechanisms to track changes in identity attributes, authentication events, and access modifications. Security Information and Event Management (SIEM) solutions can help detect anomalies in identity data, such as sudden privilege escalations or unauthorized account modifications. Regular audits of identity records can help organizations identify discrepancies, enforce compliance, and enhance overall security posture.

Another major aspect of identity data integrity is securing identity data at rest and in transit. Sensitive identity attributes, such as passwords, multi-factor authentication tokens, and biometric data, must be protected against unauthorized access and tampering. Encryption, hashing, and tokenization are essential techniques for securing identity data. Organizations should also implement strong access controls to prevent unauthorized modifications to identity records. Role-based access control (RBAC) and attribute-based access control (ABAC) help ensure that only authorized users can modify or access sensitive identity data.

Data reconciliation is a crucial practice for maintaining identity integrity across disparate systems. Organizations often acquire new platforms, migrate to cloud services, or integrate with third-party applications, leading to potential data mismatches. Identity reconciliation processes help align user attributes across different identity stores, eliminating inconsistencies. These processes involve comparing identity records, identifying conflicts, and applying rules to merge or correct discrepancies. Automated reconciliation tools can help organizations maintain a unified and accurate identity database.

Regulatory compliance further emphasizes the importance of managing identity data integrity. Regulations such as GDPR, HIPAA, and SOC 2 mandate strict controls over identity data management, requiring organizations to implement measures for data accuracy, access control, and auditability. Failure to maintain identity integrity can result in compliance violations, legal consequences, and reputational damage. Implementing identity governance frameworks ensures that organizations meet regulatory requirements while reducing security risks.

Identity data integrity also plays a role in enabling Zero Trust security models. In a Zero Trust architecture, continuous verification of user identities is required before granting access to sensitive resources. Ensuring that identity attributes are accurate and up to date enables organizations to enforce risk-based authentication and access policies. Zero Trust models rely on identity analytics and continuous monitoring to detect suspicious behavior and unauthorized identity modifications.

Advancements in artificial intelligence (AI) and machine learning (ML) are improving identity data integrity by enabling intelligent anomaly detection and automated data corrections. AI-driven identity analytics can identify patterns of inconsistencies, detect compromised accounts, and enhance identity verification processes. By leveraging AI, organizations can proactively address identity data integrity issues and reduce manual intervention.

Organizations must take a proactive approach to managing identity data integrity by implementing automated tools, enforcing strict data governance policies, and continuously monitoring identity records. By maintaining accurate, consistent, and secure identity data, businesses can improve security, streamline access management, and meet regulatory requirements. Identity data integrity is not only essential for reducing security risks but also for enabling seamless user experiences and efficient IT operations.

Securing APIs for Identity Management

APIs play a crucial role in modern identity management, enabling secure communication between identity providers, authentication services, and applications. As organizations adopt cloud-based identity solutions and federated authentication models, APIs serve as the backbone for integrating identity services across diverse platforms. However, APIs also present security challenges, as they are frequent targets for cyberattacks. Ensuring the security of APIs in identity management is essential to protect sensitive user data, prevent unauthorized access, and maintain compliance with regulatory requirements.

APIs used in identity management facilitate authentication, authorization, user provisioning, and identity synchronization. These APIs connect identity providers with applications, allowing for seamless user access and enforcing security policies. Common identity management protocols such as OAuth 2.0, OpenID Connect, and SAML depend on APIs to exchange authentication and authorization data securely. When improperly secured, these APIs can be exploited by attackers to gain unauthorized access, manipulate authentication flows, or extract user credentials.

One of the most significant security risks associated with identity management APIs is improper authentication and authorization. APIs must enforce strong authentication mechanisms to ensure that only legitimate clients and users can access identity-related data. Implementing OAuth 2.0 with properly configured scopes and access tokens ensures that API requests are authorized based on predefined security policies. OpenID Connect further enhances security by providing identity verification capabilities, allowing applications to validate user identities without exposing credentials.

API keys, tokens, and credentials must be securely managed to prevent unauthorized access. Hardcoding API keys in applications or storing them in publicly accessible repositories can lead to credential leakage, enabling attackers to exploit APIs. Organizations should adopt best practices such as storing credentials securely in environment variables, using secret management tools, and implementing automated key rotation. Additionally, tokens should have short expiration times to minimize the risk of misuse in the event of a breach.

Encryption is a fundamental security measure for protecting identity-related API communications. All API requests and responses should be transmitted over HTTPS using TLS encryption to prevent data interception and man-in-the-middle attacks. Sensitive identity attributes, such as passwords and authentication tokens, should be encrypted at rest and in transit. Implementing payload encryption for

API responses further enhances data security, ensuring that even if data is exposed, it remains unreadable without decryption keys.

Rate limiting and anomaly detection are essential techniques for protecting identity management APIs from abuse and cyberattacks. Attackers often attempt brute-force attacks, credential stuffing, and API scraping to gain unauthorized access to identity systems. Rate limiting restricts the number of API requests per user or IP address, preventing automated attacks. Anomaly detection systems monitor API traffic for unusual patterns, such as excessive failed login attempts or requests from unexpected geolocations, triggering alerts or automated responses to mitigate threats.

Identity management APIs must also enforce robust access controls to prevent unauthorized actions. Role-Based Access Control (RBAC) and Attribute-Based Access Control (ABAC) enable fine-grained permissions, ensuring that users and applications can only perform authorized actions. For example, an API handling user provisioning should restrict access to administrative users only, while read-only APIs should prevent modification of identity records. Implementing the principle of least privilege reduces the risk of unauthorized API interactions and minimizes potential attack vectors.

Auditing and logging API activity is essential for maintaining security visibility and ensuring compliance. Organizations should maintain detailed logs of API requests, including authentication attempts, authorization decisions, and changes to identity records. Centralized logging solutions and Security Information and Event Management (SIEM) platforms help security teams analyze API activity, detect anomalies, and investigate security incidents. Logs should be protected from tampering and retained according to compliance requirements, ensuring traceability in case of audits or forensic investigations.

Multi-factor authentication (MFA) can further enhance API security by requiring additional verification steps before granting access to sensitive identity services. APIs handling user authentication or privilege escalations should enforce MFA to reduce the risk of compromised credentials being exploited. Adaptive authentication mechanisms can also be implemented, adjusting authentication requirements based on risk factors such as device type, location, or behavior anomalies.

Zero Trust security principles should be applied to identity management APIs to ensure continuous verification of users and applications. Instead of granting implicit trust to API consumers based on network location or IP addresses, Zero Trust models enforce strict authentication and authorization checks for every API request. Continuous risk assessments and dynamic policy enforcement enhance API security by adapting to changing threats and reducing attack surfaces.

Organizations must also consider compliance requirements when securing identity management APIs. Regulations such as GDPR, CCPA, and HIPAA impose strict guidelines for protecting user data and identity-related information. API security measures must align with these regulations to prevent data breaches, ensure user privacy, and maintain legal compliance. Implementing data minimization strategies, user consent mechanisms, and secure audit trails helps organizations meet regulatory obligations while enhancing API security.

As cyber threats evolve, securing APIs for identity management requires a proactive approach, combining authentication best practices, encryption, access controls, and continuous monitoring. Organizations must regularly assess their API security posture, conduct penetration testing, and update security policies to address emerging risks. By implementing strong security measures, businesses can protect identity management APIs from attacks, safeguard user identities, and maintain trust in their digital ecosystems.

Cloud Identity Service Providers Overview

Cloud identity service providers play a pivotal role in modern digital infrastructure, offering scalable, secure, and flexible solutions for managing user identities and access across diverse platforms. These providers have emerged as essential partners for organizations navigating the complexities of cloud-first strategies, multi-cloud environments, and hybrid IT landscapes. By centralizing authentication, streamlining user management, and enabling secure collaboration, cloud identity service providers help businesses maintain control over their digital assets while enhancing user experience and compliance.

At their core, cloud identity service providers deliver Identity-as-a-Service (IDaaS) solutions that replace traditional on-premises identity management infrastructure. This shift allows organizations to leverage the scalability of the cloud, reduce infrastructure maintenance costs, and ensure continuous updates and security enhancements. IDaaS platforms handle critical functions such as user provisioning, single sign-on (SSO), multi-factor authentication (MFA), directory synchronization, and access governance. By outsourcing these responsibilities to cloud identity service providers, organizations can focus on their core business objectives while leaving the complexities of identity management to the experts.

One of the key benefits of working with cloud identity service providers is their ability to unify identity management across multiple cloud platforms and on-premises systems. Modern businesses often rely on a mix of software-as-a-service (SaaS) applications, infrastructure-as-a-service (IaaS) solutions, and legacy on-premises applications. Managing identities and access independently for each platform can lead to inconsistencies, security gaps, and administrative overhead. Cloud identity service providers offer centralized authentication frameworks, enabling seamless user access and consistent policy enforcement regardless of the underlying infrastructure.

Security is a primary driver for adopting cloud identity service providers. As cyber threats grow in sophistication, organizations need robust authentication and access control mechanisms. Leading providers incorporate advanced security features such as risk-based authentication, adaptive access policies, and machine learning-driven threat detection. They also support compliance with regulatory frameworks like GDPR, HIPAA, and SOC 2 by providing detailed audit logs, granular access controls, and automated compliance reporting. These security and compliance features not only help protect sensitive data but also give organizations the confidence to adopt cloud-based technologies without compromising security.

Scalability is another critical advantage offered by cloud identity service providers. As organizations grow or experience fluctuations in their workforce, the ability to scale identity services up or down without extensive infrastructure changes is invaluable. Cloud-based identity platforms handle increasing user loads, accommodate new applications, and integrate with third-party solutions without the need for significant capital investment. This elasticity allows businesses to respond quickly to changing demands, whether they are expanding to new regions, onboarding seasonal workers, or integrating newly acquired companies.

Integration and interoperability are essential aspects of cloud identity service providers' value proposition. These providers typically support industry standards such as Security Assertion Markup Language (SAML), OpenID Connect (OIDC), and OAuth 2.0, ensuring that their solutions can work seamlessly with a wide range of applications and services. In addition, they offer APIs and developer tools that enable organizations to customize identity workflows, build custom integrations, and extend identity capabilities to meet unique business requirements. By supporting standard protocols and providing flexible integration options, cloud identity service providers help organizations create a unified and secure identity ecosystem.

User experience is a critical factor in identity management, and cloud identity service providers excel at delivering frictionless access for end users. Single sign-on (SSO) functionality reduces password fatigue by allowing users to access multiple applications with a single set of credentials. Self-service portals empower users to manage their own accounts, reset passwords, and request additional access without involving IT support. Multi-factor authentication (MFA) enhances security without disrupting user workflows, and adaptive authentication adjusts requirements based on risk factors, providing a seamless yet secure login experience. By prioritizing user experience, cloud identity service providers improve productivity and satisfaction while maintaining stringent security standards.

For organizations operating in hybrid and multi-cloud environments, cloud identity service providers simplify the complexities of managing identities across disparate platforms. They bridge the gap between on-premises directories and cloud-based identity solutions, enabling consistent authentication and access policies. This integration reduces the need for multiple, disconnected identity systems and provides a unified view of users, devices, and access rights. As businesses increasingly adopt multi-cloud strategies, the ability to manage identities centrally becomes even more critical, and cloud identity service providers are well-positioned to meet this need.

In addition to their core services, many cloud identity service providers offer advanced analytics and reporting capabilities. Identity analytics helps organizations identify unusual behavior, detect potential security threats, and optimize access policies. Detailed reporting enables administrators to monitor user activity, track access changes, and demonstrate compliance with internal and external requirements. By providing actionable insights and visibility into identity-related activities, cloud identity service providers help organizations make informed decisions and maintain a proactive security posture.

Cloud identity service providers are also driving innovation in the identity space, incorporating emerging technologies such as artificial intelligence (AI) and machine learning (ML) to enhance their offerings. AI-powered identity solutions can detect anomalies, automate identity lifecycle management, and improve threat detection. Machine learning models can continuously learn from authentication patterns, reducing false positives and improving the accuracy of risk assessments. These advancements enable cloud identity service providers to stay ahead of evolving threats and deliver more secure and efficient identity management solutions.

As organizations continue their digital transformation journeys, the role of cloud identity service providers will only grow in importance. By offering scalable, secure, and user-friendly identity solutions, these providers help businesses navigate the complexities of modern IT environments. Whether it's enabling seamless access to cloud applications, supporting compliance efforts, or enhancing security with advanced analytics, cloud identity service providers are essential partners for organizations seeking to manage identities effectively in a rapidly changing digital landscape.

Building a Scalable Identity Architecture

A scalable identity architecture is essential for organizations navigating the complexities of digital transformation, cloud adoption, and evolving security threats. As businesses grow, so does the number of users, devices, and applications they must manage. Without a well-designed identity architecture, this growth can quickly lead to inefficiencies, security gaps, and operational challenges. By building a scalable identity framework, organizations ensure that their identity systems can handle increasing demands while maintaining security, efficiency, and user satisfaction.

Scalability in identity architecture involves more than just adding capacity. It requires designing systems and processes that can accommodate growth without significant redesign or administrative overhead. A key consideration is ensuring that identity data remains consistent and synchronized across all environments. In many organizations, identity information is stored in multiple directories, cloud identity providers, and application-specific databases. A scalable architecture must seamlessly integrate these sources, allowing users to access resources regardless of where their identities originate. This unified approach simplifies user provisioning, enhances security, and improves overall efficiency.

One of the foundational elements of a scalable identity architecture is the adoption of standardized protocols and frameworks. Standards like Security Assertion Markup Language (SAML), OpenID Connect, and OAuth provide a consistent foundation for authentication and authorization. By using widely accepted standards, organizations can ensure interoperability between different identity providers, applications, and cloud platforms. This approach not only simplifies integration but also reduces the risk of vendor lock-in, allowing businesses to scale their identity systems without being tied to a single provider or technology stack.

Another important aspect of scalability is automation. Manual identity processes become increasingly unsustainable as organizations grow. Automating identity lifecycle management—such as provisioning, deprovisioning, and access reviews—reduces administrative overhead, minimizes human error, and ensures that users have the right level of access at all times. Automation also allows for rapid onboarding of new employees, contractors, or partners, which is critical during periods of growth or mergers and acquisitions. With an automated, policy-driven approach, organizations can maintain consistent security policies and streamline compliance efforts even as their user base expands.

Cloud identity solutions play a crucial role in building scalable architectures. Unlike traditional on-premises identity systems, cloud-based identity platforms offer the flexibility to scale up or down as needed. They provide built-in redundancy, high availability, and global coverage, ensuring that users can access resources from anywhere in the world without performance degradation. Moreover, cloud identity services integrate easily with multiple SaaS applications and infrastructure providers, making it easier to manage identities across a diverse IT environment. By leveraging the cloud, organizations can handle spikes in usage, support a distributed workforce, and maintain a consistent security posture.

Performance and reliability are also critical considerations when designing a scalable identity architecture. As the number of authentication requests and access decisions increases, identity systems must remain responsive to avoid slowing down user workflows. Load balancing, caching, and distributed directory architectures help maintain performance under heavy loads. Additionally, implementing monitoring and alerting mechanisms allows organizations to identify bottlenecks, address issues proactively, and ensure that their identity infrastructure can handle growing demands without disruption.

Security remains a top priority when scaling identity architectures. As the number of users and connected systems grows, so does the attack surface. A scalable identity framework must incorporate robust security measures, including multi-factor authentication, adaptive risk-based policies, and continuous monitoring for anomalies. By embedding security into the architecture from the start, organizations can scale without compromising the integrity of their identity systems. Furthermore, integrating advanced threat detection technologies, such as artificial intelligence and machine learning, enhances the ability to identify and respond to emerging threats as the environment grows.

Compliance and regulatory requirements also shape the design of scalable identity architectures. As businesses expand, they often operate in multiple regions, each with its own data protection laws and industry standards. A scalable identity framework must support diverse compliance mandates, providing detailed audit logs, access certifications, and data residency controls. This ensures that the organization can meet regulatory obligations while maintaining a unified approach to identity management. By integrating compliance capabilities directly into the architecture, organizations reduce the complexity and cost of maintaining regulatory adherence as they grow.

User experience is another critical factor in scaling identity systems. Employees, contractors, and customers expect seamless access to resources without unnecessary friction. Single sign-on (SSO) and self-service capabilities improve productivity by reducing password fatigue and enabling users to manage their own accounts. As the organization grows, ensuring a consistent, user-friendly experience becomes even more important. A scalable identity architecture should be designed to handle large-scale user populations without degrading the quality of the user experience. This not only improves satisfaction but also increases user adoption of identity best practices, ultimately enhancing security.

Finally, building a scalable identity architecture requires a strategic, long-term approach. Organizations must anticipate future growth, emerging technologies, and evolving threat landscapes. By choosing flexible, standards-based solutions and investing in automation, cloud integration, and advanced security measures, businesses can ensure that their identity systems are ready to meet new challenges. Scalability is not just about handling more users—it's about enabling the organization to adapt and thrive in a rapidly changing digital world. With a well-designed identity architecture, companies can support growth, maintain security, and deliver seamless access to resources, empowering their workforce and protecting their critical assets.

Identity Management in Hybrid Environments

Identity management in hybrid environments has become an increasingly vital component of modern IT strategies. With the widespread adoption of cloud services, many organizations still rely on existing on-premises systems to handle core business functions. This creates a complex mix of traditional and cloud-based infrastructures, where managing user identities, securing access, and ensuring consistent policies present unique challenges. In such a scenario, identity management serves as a critical bridge, allowing organizations to seamlessly integrate on-premises directories, cloud identity providers, and various authentication mechanisms into a cohesive and secure framework.

Hybrid environments typically consist of a combination of on-premises Active Directory (AD), Lightweight Directory Access Protocol (LDAP) systems, and cloud-based identity providers like Azure AD, Okta, or Google Workspace. These infrastructures often have their own sets of authentication protocols, user directories, and access policies. Without a unified identity management strategy, organizations may find themselves with fragmented identity systems that lead to inconsistent access controls, duplicate accounts, and administrative inefficiencies. To address these challenges, hybrid identity management focuses on establishing a single source of truth for user identities, synchronizing identity attributes, and maintaining consistent policies across both on-premises and cloud platforms.

One of the most significant considerations in hybrid identity management is directory synchronization. On-premises systems often contain legacy user accounts and group memberships that must remain functional even as organizations transition to the cloud.

Directory synchronization ensures that these identities are replicated in cloud identity platforms, allowing users to authenticate with a single set of credentials. This approach reduces the need for redundant accounts and simplifies the user experience, as employees, contractors, and partners only need to remember one password. Synchronization also enables centralized policy enforcement, ensuring that security controls and compliance measures are consistently applied across all systems.

Another essential aspect of hybrid identity management is maintaining secure authentication processes. As users access both on-premises and cloud resources, organizations must implement authentication mechanisms that work seamlessly across different environments. Multi-factor authentication (MFA) is a key component in this effort, providing an additional layer of security for both traditional and cloud-based applications. Hybrid identity solutions integrate MFA into existing workflows, allowing organizations to enforce strong authentication policies without disrupting user productivity. Additionally, hybrid identity systems can leverage adaptive authentication, which adjusts authentication requirements based on risk factors like device type, location, or user behavior.

Access management also plays a crucial role in hybrid environments. Role-based access control (RBAC) and attribute-based access control (ABAC) are common approaches that ensure users only have access to the resources necessary for their job functions. In a hybrid environment, these access policies must be enforced consistently across on-premises and cloud platforms. This is often achieved through centralized identity management tools that provide a single interface for defining, monitoring, and adjusting access policies. By applying these policies uniformly, organizations can reduce the risk of unauthorized access, protect sensitive data, and streamline compliance efforts.

Hybrid identity management also supports secure collaboration between different organizations and third-party vendors. In many cases, external partners need access to internal resources, such as project management tools or document repositories. A hybrid identity solution allows organizations to extend authentication and authorization to external users without creating multiple separate accounts. Federation protocols, such as SAML and OpenID Connect, enable secure, standards-based authentication across organizational boundaries. This approach simplifies collaboration, reduces administrative overhead, and maintains strong security controls, even when dealing with external stakeholders.

Another critical consideration in hybrid environments is managing the lifecycle of user identities. Employees change roles, contractors come and go, and projects end, all of which impact user access needs. A hybrid identity management strategy must include robust provisioning and deprovisioning processes to ensure that access is granted or revoked promptly. Automating these lifecycle events reduces administrative burden and helps maintain a clean, secure identity environment. By integrating identity lifecycle management tools with both on-premises and cloud platforms, organizations can ensure that user accounts are always up-to-date, minimizing the risk of privilege creep or orphaned accounts.

Regulatory compliance and auditability are other factors that hybrid identity management must address. Many industries require organizations to maintain detailed records of who accessed what and when. A hybrid identity strategy must provide unified logging and reporting capabilities that span both on-premises and cloud environments. Security teams need comprehensive visibility into authentication attempts, access modifications, and user activity to identify potential threats and demonstrate compliance with frameworks like GDPR, HIPAA, or SOC 2. Hybrid identity solutions that offer centralized logging and advanced analytics help organizations meet these compliance requirements while strengthening their overall security posture.

As hybrid environments continue to evolve, organizations are increasingly adopting Zero Trust security models. In a Zero Trust framework, no user or device is implicitly trusted, and every access request is continuously verified. Hybrid identity management supports Zero Trust by enabling granular policy enforcement and real-time risk assessments. By integrating identity verification into every access decision, organizations can minimize lateral movement attacks, prevent unauthorized access, and respond quickly to emerging threats. Hybrid identity solutions are uniquely positioned to implement Zero

Trust principles across both legacy systems and modern cloud platforms.

Ultimately, identity management in hybrid environments requires a holistic approach that encompasses synchronization, authentication, access control, lifecycle management, and compliance. By integrating these elements into a unified strategy, organizations can maintain a secure, efficient, and flexible identity infrastructure that supports both existing on-premises systems and rapidly expanding cloud services. This ensures that users have seamless access to the resources they need while protecting sensitive data, reducing administrative complexity, and meeting the demands of an increasingly dynamic digital landscape.

Integrating On-Premises and Cloud Directories

Integrating on-premises and cloud directories is a crucial step for organizations that rely on both traditional IT infrastructure and modern cloud services. While on-premises directories like Active Directory (AD) have long been the cornerstone of identity management, the growing adoption of Software-as-a-Service (SaaS) applications and cloud platforms introduces the need for a unified, hybrid identity approach. Bridging these environments helps maintain a single source of truth for user identities, streamlines authentication processes, and enhances security by applying consistent policies across all resources.

One of the main drivers for integrating on-premises and cloud directories is the need to provide seamless access to resources. Employees, contractors, and partners increasingly expect to use a single set of credentials to access both internal systems and external cloud applications. Without integration, users may face multiple logins, inconsistent experiences, and reduced productivity. Integration ensures that identities and credentials flow seamlessly between environments, enabling users to work efficiently while maintaining robust security measures.

Synchronization is at the heart of integration efforts. By synchronizing identity attributes—such as usernames, group memberships, and passwords—between on-premises directories and cloud identity providers, organizations can create a unified identity system. Tools like Azure AD Connect, Google Cloud Directory Sync, and third-party identity management solutions help automate this synchronization process. These tools ensure that changes made in the on-premises directory, such as a new hire's account creation or a departing employee's account removal, are reflected in the cloud environment in near real-time. This reduces administrative overhead, improves consistency, and helps maintain a single source of truth for identity data.

Another key benefit of integration is the ability to extend familiar security and compliance policies to cloud resources. Many organizations have invested years in refining their on-premises directory structures, implementing group policies, and enforcing access controls. By integrating on-premises directories with cloud directories, businesses can leverage these existing policies in a hybrid environment. For instance, group memberships defined in Active Directory can be used to control access to SaaS applications, ensuring that employees only have access to the resources they need. This continuity simplifies compliance audits, enhances security, and allows IT teams to apply a consistent governance framework across all platforms.

Integration also supports single sign-on (SSO) capabilities. SSO enables users to authenticate once and gain access to multiple applications and services without repeatedly entering credentials. By connecting on-premises directories to cloud identity providers, organizations can offer SSO experiences that span internal systems and external cloud applications. This not only improves the user experience but also reduces the likelihood of password fatigue and the associated security risks, such as weak passwords or password reuse. Additionally, SSO simplifies user lifecycle management, as access can be automatically updated or revoked through a single identity source.

Multi-factor authentication (MFA) is another critical security measure that benefits from directory integration. MFA adds an extra layer of protection by requiring users to verify their identity with something they have (such as a mobile phone or hardware token) in addition to something they know (like a password). Integrating on-premises directories with cloud identity platforms enables consistent MFA enforcement across all resources, whether users are accessing a legacy internal system or a cloud-based SaaS application. This uniform approach enhances security by applying strong authentication policies regardless of the environment.

A common challenge in integrating directories is ensuring compatibility between different directory schemas and authentication protocols. On-premises directories often use older standards, while cloud identity providers rely on modern, lightweight protocols. Integration solutions must bridge these differences by translating attributes, mapping group memberships, and supporting standards like LDAP, SAML, OAuth, and OpenID Connect. By using standards-based approaches and leveraging tools designed for interoperability, organizations can overcome these technical challenges and create a seamless identity environment.

Performance and reliability are critical considerations when integrating directories. A well-integrated hybrid identity system should ensure that authentication and authorization requests are handled quickly and reliably. This often requires deploying hybrid identity connectors in multiple locations to provide redundancy and reduce latency. By ensuring that directory integration tools are configured for high availability, organizations can maintain a seamless user experience even during unexpected outages or high-traffic periods.

Data residency and compliance also influence directory integration strategies. Certain industries and regions have strict requirements for where identity data can be stored and processed. Integrating on-premises and cloud directories allows organizations to enforce data residency policies by keeping sensitive information on-premises while still benefiting from the flexibility and scalability of cloud-based identity services. Additionally, hybrid integration helps organizations maintain detailed audit trails and compliance records, which are critical for demonstrating adherence to regulatory frameworks.

As identity management evolves, the integration of on-premises and cloud directories is becoming increasingly sophisticated. Artificial intelligence (AI) and machine learning (ML) are being integrated into identity platforms to enhance identity analytics, detect anomalies, and automate policy enforcement. These advancements help organizations optimize their hybrid identity environments, improving security and efficiency while reducing manual administrative tasks.

Integrating on-premises and cloud directories is not just a technical necessity but also a strategic enabler. By creating a unified identity system that spans traditional and modern environments, organizations can improve user experience, strengthen security, and maintain a consistent governance framework. This integration is the foundation of a hybrid identity approach that ensures seamless access, robust compliance, and efficient identity lifecycle management, all while supporting the organization's broader digital transformation goals.

Identity Standards: SAML, OAuth, OpenID Connect

As the demand for secure, seamless user authentication grows, identity standards like SAML, OAuth, and OpenID Connect have become essential tools for managing identities across diverse platforms and services. These protocols establish a common language for authentication and authorization, enabling secure communication between identity providers (IdPs) and service providers (SPs) while eliminating the need for proprietary solutions. By implementing these widely adopted standards, organizations can ensure interoperability, enhance security, and provide a better user experience.

Security Assertion Markup Language (SAML) is one of the oldest and most widely used identity standards. Introduced in the early 2000s,

SAML provides a framework for exchanging authentication and authorization data between IdPs and SPs. It is an XML-based protocol that allows users to sign in once with their IdP credentials and gain access to multiple SPs without re-entering credentials. This single sign-on (SSO) functionality is a major advantage of SAML, as it reduces password fatigue, strengthens security by centralizing authentication, and simplifies the user experience. SAML's ability to work with established on-premises directories like Active Directory makes it a common choice for organizations transitioning to a hybrid or cloud environment.

SAML operates through a series of assertions that communicate user authentication status and access permissions. When a user attempts to access a service, the SP redirects them to the IdP. The IdP authenticates the user and sends a SAML assertion to the SP, verifying the user's identity. The SP then grants or denies access based on the assertion. This process ensures that authentication details remain secure, as the user's credentials are never directly shared with the SP. SAML's strong encryption and robust signing mechanisms help protect against attacks, making it a reliable choice for many enterprise environments.

OAuth, introduced several years after SAML, focuses on authorization rather than authentication. It allows users to grant third-party applications limited access to their resources without sharing their credentials. For example, a user might authorize a social media app to post on their behalf without giving the app their login password. OAuth achieves this by issuing access tokens—temporary, limited-use credentials that applications can present to resource servers. This token-based approach simplifies integration between services and improves security by reducing the need to handle user passwords directly.

OAuth's flexibility has made it a cornerstone for many modern applications and services. It supports a range of use cases, from authorizing mobile apps and APIs to enabling access for IoT devices. By separating resource owners, clients, and authorization servers, OAuth creates a clear security model that can adapt to various scenarios. For example, a mobile banking app might use OAuth to grant access to a user's financial data on a bank's servers, while still maintaining strict control over what actions the app can perform. This level of granularity ensures that users remain in control of their data and that third-party apps only have the permissions they truly need.

OpenID Connect (OIDC) builds on OAuth's foundation by adding a standardized layer for user authentication. While OAuth primarily handles authorization, OIDC extends it to provide identity verification. This allows developers to use OAuth's token-based model to authenticate users and retrieve their identity information, such as their name, email address, and unique identifier. OIDC's design makes it especially well-suited for single sign-on scenarios in modern web and mobile applications. By using the same underlying framework as OAuth, OIDC ensures compatibility and simplicity while delivering a more complete identity solution.

One of OIDC's key features is its reliance on JSON Web Tokens (JWTs). These compact, URL-safe tokens carry claims about the user's identity and can be easily validated by the relying party (the application requesting authentication). JWTs simplify the process of transmitting user information and reduce the overhead associated with traditional XML-based protocols like SAML. This lightweight design has contributed to OIDC's popularity, particularly in scenarios where performance and ease of implementation are crucial.

The adoption of these identity standards—SAML, OAuth, and OIDC—has significantly improved interoperability across diverse systems. By providing common frameworks and well-defined workflows, these protocols ensure that identity providers, service providers, and applications can work together regardless of their underlying technologies. This interoperability is particularly important in hybrid and multi-cloud environments, where organizations need to integrate on-premises directories, cloud identity providers, and third-party applications seamlessly. Using standards-based approaches eliminates vendor lock-in, reduces complexity, and enables organizations to adapt to new technologies more easily.

Security is another major advantage of these identity standards. SAML's strong encryption and digital signing mechanisms protect authentication data from tampering and interception. OAuth's token-based model minimizes the exposure of user credentials and allows for fine-grained access controls. OIDC's integration of authentication with

OAuth simplifies the process of verifying user identities, reducing the risk of phishing attacks and credential theft. By relying on well-established standards, organizations can leverage proven security best practices rather than developing their own, potentially flawed, solutions.

Finally, these identity standards contribute to a better user experience. SAML's SSO capabilities reduce the need for multiple logins, while OAuth's delegated authorization model allows users to connect services without sharing passwords. OIDC further enhances this experience by enabling seamless authentication and identity retrieval across applications. These improvements not only simplify users' workflows but also increase adoption and engagement, as users are more likely to trust and use systems that provide smooth, secure access.

SAML, OAuth, and OpenID Connect have become essential components of modern identity and access management. Their widespread adoption, strong security foundations, and ability to integrate diverse systems make them critical tools for organizations seeking to streamline authentication, improve user experience, and protect sensitive data. As businesses continue to embrace digital transformation and cloud-first strategies, these identity standards will remain central to creating secure, scalable, and user-friendly identity frameworks.

Passwordless Authentication Approaches

Passwordless authentication is rapidly emerging as a solution to some of the biggest challenges in identity and access management. Traditional password-based systems have long been a source of frustration for users and a weak point in security. People often choose simple, easily guessable passwords, reuse credentials across multiple sites, and fall victim to phishing attacks. As organizations seek to enhance security and improve the user experience, passwordless authentication approaches are gaining traction. By eliminating passwords altogether, these methods reduce the attack surface, increase convenience, and help ensure a more secure authentication process.

One common passwordless approach is the use of biometrics. Biometric authentication relies on unique physical or behavioral traits, such as fingerprints, facial recognition, or voice patterns, to verify identity. Modern smartphones and laptops often come equipped with built-in biometric sensors, making this method both convenient and widely accessible. Unlike passwords, biometrics are difficult to steal or replicate, adding a layer of security that is both user-friendly and effective. By using biometrics, organizations can provide a seamless authentication experience that eliminates the need for users to remember or manage complex passwords.

Another increasingly popular method is the use of physical security keys. These small hardware tokens, often referred to as FIDO (Fast Identity Online) keys, enable strong passwordless authentication by generating cryptographic credentials that are stored on the device. When a user needs to authenticate, they simply plug the key into a USB port or tap it against a device using near-field communication (NFC). The key then performs a cryptographic handshake with the service, verifying the user's identity without the need for a password. Because the credentials never leave the device and are not shared with the service, security keys offer strong protection against phishing and other attacks.

Device-based authentication is another common passwordless approach. This method leverages trusted devices, such as smartphones or laptops, to confirm user identity. For instance, a user might receive a push notification on their phone or be prompted to use their device's built-in biometric sensor. The device acts as a secure token, allowing the user to access resources without entering a password. This type of authentication is not only more secure but also reduces friction, as users already carry their trusted devices with them and can authenticate in seconds.

Smartcards and similar token-based systems also offer passwordless authentication. These cards store cryptographic credentials and often require a PIN or a fingerprint to activate. Once activated, the smartcard can securely authenticate the user to services, providing a strong, password-free login experience. Smartcards are commonly used in government and highly regulated industries where stringent security standards are required. While they may involve an upfront investment in hardware and infrastructure, smartcards provide robust protection against unauthorized access and credential theft.

One of the most innovative approaches to passwordless authentication is risk-based authentication. This method evaluates various factors—such as the user's location, device type, login history, and behavioral patterns—to determine whether additional verification is needed. If the login attempt appears low-risk, the user may be granted access without providing a password or even a second factor. If the system detects unusual activity, it can prompt the user to verify their identity through another means, such as a biometric scan or a temporary code. By dynamically adjusting the authentication process, risk-based authentication enhances security while maintaining a frictionless experience for legitimate users.

Passkeys are a newer form of passwordless authentication that leverage cryptographic keys stored on user devices. Instead of relying on traditional passwords, passkeys are bound to the user's hardware and are used to securely log in to applications and websites. When a user needs to authenticate, the passkey is matched against the service's stored public key, and the user gains access without ever entering a password. This approach not only reduces password-related security risks but also simplifies account recovery and improves the overall login experience.

Passwordless authentication approaches also integrate well with multi-factor authentication (MFA). By combining passwordless methods with additional security layers, such as biometrics or security tokens, organizations can create a more robust authentication framework. For example, a user might authenticate with a fingerprint on a registered device and then confirm their login attempt via a push notification. This combination of factors enhances security while still eliminating the need for traditional passwords.

Implementing passwordless authentication requires careful planning and integration. Organizations must ensure that their chosen methods are compatible with existing identity management infrastructure and that they provide a seamless experience across all devices and platforms. It's also important to educate users about how passwordless authentication works and the benefits it provides. User adoption is critical to success, so clear communication and straightforward onboarding processes are key.

As the digital landscape evolves, passwordless authentication approaches offer a way to enhance security, improve user experience, and reduce the administrative burden of managing passwords. By leveraging biometrics, security keys, device-based methods, and other innovative technologies, organizations can move beyond the limitations of traditional password systems. These approaches not only mitigate common attack vectors but also pave the way for a more secure and user-friendly future in authentication.

Risk-Based Authentication and Adaptive Security

In an increasingly complex threat landscape, traditional authentication methods are no longer sufficient to protect digital assets. Passwords, even when paired with two-factor authentication, can be compromised, leaving systems vulnerable to unauthorized access. Risk-based authentication and adaptive security offer a more dynamic approach to safeguarding identities and resources. By continuously evaluating the risk associated with each login attempt or user action, these methods provide an intelligent and responsive layer of security that adjusts to the context of the interaction.

Risk-based authentication focuses on assessing various factors that may indicate whether an access request is legitimate or potentially malicious. These factors include the user's location, device type, IP address, login history, and behavioral patterns. For instance, if an employee typically logs in from a specific city using a corporate laptop but suddenly attempts to log in from an unfamiliar country on an unrecognized device, the system flags the attempt as higher risk. Rather than relying on static credentials alone, risk-based authentication uses these contextual signals to determine whether additional verification steps are necessary.

Adaptive security builds on this concept by dynamically adjusting the level of authentication required based on the assessed risk. If the system detects no anomalies—such as a user logging in from a known device and a familiar location—it may allow access with minimal friction. However, if the system identifies unusual behavior, it can prompt the user for additional factors, such as a one-time code sent to a mobile device, a biometric scan, or a push notification approval. By tailoring the authentication experience to the risk level, adaptive security enhances both usability and protection.

One of the key benefits of risk-based authentication and adaptive security is their ability to reduce user friction without compromising security. Traditional approaches often apply the same authentication requirements to all users, regardless of the context. This can lead to frustration, as users are forced to repeatedly verify their identities even in low-risk scenarios. Adaptive security changes this dynamic by applying stringent checks only when the risk is elevated. As a result, legitimate users enjoy a smoother experience, while potential attackers face additional barriers that make unauthorized access more difficult.

Another advantage is the ability to stay ahead of evolving threats. Cybercriminals are constantly developing new tactics, such as phishing campaigns, credential stuffing, and social engineering attacks. Static authentication methods struggle to keep up with these changing threat vectors. Risk-based authentication, however, leverages real-time data and advanced analytics to identify and respond to suspicious activities as they occur. Machine learning and artificial intelligence play a significant role in enhancing these capabilities. By analyzing large volumes of data, AI models can detect subtle patterns and anomalies that may indicate fraudulent behavior, enabling organizations to respond quickly to emerging threats.

Implementing risk-based authentication and adaptive security requires a combination of technologies and processes. Organizations must first gather and analyze contextual data from various sources, including user devices, network activity, and historical login records. This data is then fed into risk engines that assign a risk score to each access request. Based on the score, the system determines the appropriate authentication measures to apply. Over time, these risk engines learn from new data, improving their accuracy and effectiveness.

It is also essential to define clear risk policies and thresholds. Security teams must establish criteria for what constitutes low, medium, and high-risk scenarios, as well as the corresponding authentication steps. For example, a low-risk login might only require a username and password, while a high-risk attempt could trigger a series of additional verifications, such as MFA and manual approval by an administrator. By codifying these policies, organizations ensure that the adaptive security system operates consistently and effectively.

User education and communication are also critical to the success of these approaches. Employees, partners, and customers need to understand why additional authentication steps are sometimes required and how these measures protect their accounts and sensitive data. Clear messaging helps build trust and reduces pushback from users who might otherwise view extra security steps as inconvenient. By framing adaptive security as a proactive measure to protect their identities, organizations can encourage acceptance and compliance.

Regulatory and compliance considerations further underscore the importance of risk-based authentication and adaptive security. Many industries face stringent requirements for access controls, data protection, and audit trails. Adaptive security frameworks help organizations meet these standards by providing detailed logs of authentication events, risk assessments, and policy enforcement. In the event of a compliance audit or security investigation, these records demonstrate that the organization has implemented robust, context-aware security measures.

As technology evolves, risk-based authentication and adaptive security will continue to play a central role in identity management strategies. By moving beyond static, one-size-fits-all authentication models, these approaches deliver a more responsive, flexible, and effective means of protecting digital resources. Organizations that embrace risk-based and adaptive methods can better defend against modern cyber threats, reduce user friction, and maintain a strong security posture in an ever-changing environment.

Identity Analytics and Reporting

Identity analytics and reporting have become indispensable tools for modern organizations seeking to maintain robust security, streamline access management, and meet compliance requirements. With the rise of cloud computing, mobile workforces, and sophisticated cyber threats, tracking and understanding identity-related activities is more critical than ever. Identity analytics leverages advanced technologies, including machine learning and data visualization, to provide actionable insights into user behavior, access patterns, and potential risks. By combining these insights with comprehensive reporting capabilities, organizations can strengthen their identity governance frameworks and reduce the likelihood of security breaches.

At the core of identity analytics is the ability to aggregate and analyze identity data from multiple sources. Organizations typically maintain identities across various systems, including on-premises directories, cloud-based identity providers, SaaS applications, and internal databases. Each of these systems generates a wealth of information, from login attempts and access requests to privilege assignments and group memberships. Identity analytics tools consolidate this data, creating a centralized repository that can be queried, visualized, and used to identify trends and anomalies. This holistic view is essential for understanding how identities are used and where security or compliance gaps may exist.

One of the key benefits of identity analytics is its capacity to detect abnormal or risky behavior. Traditional identity and access management (IAM) solutions often rely on predefined rules or policies to determine what constitutes normal activity. However, this approach can miss emerging threats that do not fit existing patterns. Identity analytics employs machine learning algorithms to analyze historical data and build behavioral baselines for users and devices. Once these baselines are established, the system can flag deviations in real time. For example, if an employee who typically logs in from a single office location suddenly attempts to access sensitive data from multiple international locations, identity analytics tools can trigger alerts and prompt further investigation.

Another valuable application of identity analytics is the detection of privilege creep. Over time, users often accumulate permissions that exceed what is necessary for their roles. This can occur when employees switch departments, temporarily take on additional responsibilities, or when access reviews are not conducted regularly. Identity analytics helps identify users whose current access privileges do not align with their current roles or job functions. By pinpointing these discrepancies, organizations can adjust permissions, enforce least-privilege access, and reduce the risk of insider threats.

Comprehensive reporting is another critical component of identity governance. Regulatory frameworks such as GDPR, HIPAA, and SOX require organizations to maintain detailed records of identity and access activities. Identity reporting tools generate audit-ready logs that track who accessed what, when, and how. These logs provide transparency and accountability, allowing organizations to demonstrate compliance during audits and security reviews. Furthermore, reports can highlight areas where policies need improvement, such as excessive privilege assignments or frequent failed login attempts, enabling security teams to address these issues proactively.

Identity reporting also plays a crucial role in incident response. When a security incident occurs, organizations must quickly determine how the breach happened and which accounts were involved. Detailed identity logs enable rapid forensic analysis, helping investigators trace the attack's origin, identify affected resources, and understand the attacker's methods. With clear, comprehensive reports, security teams can respond more effectively, minimize damage, and prevent similar incidents in the future.

In addition to enhancing security and compliance, identity analytics and reporting contribute to better decision-making. By providing data-driven insights into user behavior and access patterns, these tools help IT and security leaders allocate resources more effectively. For example, identity analytics might reveal that a significant percentage of help desk tickets involve password resets, prompting the implementation of self-service password recovery solutions. Similarly, analytics may show that certain departments frequently request new application access, indicating a need for more streamlined provisioning processes. These insights enable organizations to optimize workflows, reduce administrative overhead, and improve overall operational efficiency.

Modern identity analytics platforms increasingly incorporate artificial intelligence (AI) and machine learning capabilities to refine their analysis and provide more accurate insights. These technologies allow systems to adapt to changing user behavior, detect subtle anomalies, and even predict potential risks before they occur. By continuously learning from new data, AI-powered identity analytics tools improve over time, offering organizations a more proactive approach to identity governance.

Another emerging trend in identity analytics is the use of intuitive dashboards and visualization tools. Raw data can be overwhelming, but visualizing trends and anomalies through graphs, charts, and heatmaps makes it easier for security teams to understand the current identity landscape. Dashboards that display key performance indicators (KPIs) related to access requests, privilege changes, and policy violations provide at-a-glance insights that inform decision-making. These visual tools also facilitate communication between technical and non-technical stakeholders, ensuring that everyone in the organization understands the importance of identity governance.

Identity analytics and reporting are essential components of a modern identity management strategy. By consolidating identity data, detecting anomalous behavior, generating detailed compliance reports, and providing actionable insights, these tools empower organizations to strengthen their security posture, streamline operations, and meet regulatory requirements. As identity-related risks continue to evolve, investing in robust identity analytics and reporting capabilities will remain a top priority for organizations seeking to protect their digital assets and maintain trust with their users.

Enhancing User Experience with Modern Authentication

Modern authentication technologies have transformed the way users interact with digital systems, providing both improved security and a streamlined user experience. In today's fast-paced, digitally connected world, the expectation is clear: users want seamless, secure, and efficient ways to access applications and services. Modern authentication methods—such as biometrics, single sign-on (SSO), and passwordless approaches—offer organizations the ability to meet these expectations while reducing friction and maintaining strong security postures. By focusing on user-centric authentication strategies, companies can enhance productivity, foster trust, and ensure a smoother overall experience for employees, customers, and partners.

One key development in modern authentication is the use of biometrics. Fingerprints, facial recognition, and even voice patterns allow users to authenticate quickly and conveniently, without needing to remember complex passwords or carry multiple tokens. Mobile devices and laptops now commonly feature built-in biometric sensors, making this approach widely accessible. Biometric authentication reduces the risk of password-based attacks and simplifies the login process. For users, it means fewer barriers to accessing their accounts and a more natural way to verify their identities.

Single sign-on (SSO) is another significant advancement that improves the user experience. With SSO, users only need to authenticate once to gain access to multiple systems and applications. This eliminates the frustration of managing numerous passwords and logging in repeatedly. SSO not only reduces the cognitive load on users but also saves time, especially in workplaces where employees rely on dozens of tools and services throughout the day. By centralizing authentication through a trusted identity provider, organizations can ensure a consistent, secure, and frictionless experience for all users.

Passwordless authentication takes these improvements even further by removing passwords from the equation entirely. Instead, users authenticate through methods such as device-based tokens, push notifications, or biometric scans. This approach significantly reduces the risk of phishing and credential theft while providing a smoother login process. For instance, a user can simply tap a security key or approve a login request on their phone, bypassing the need to remember or type in a password. By adopting passwordless methods, organizations not only enhance security but also deliver a more user-friendly authentication experience.

Another important aspect of modern authentication is adaptive authentication. Rather than treating all login attempts the same, adaptive authentication evaluates the context of each request. Factors such as the user's location, device, time of access, and behavior patterns influence the level of authentication required. For example, if a user logs in from a known device at their usual location, the system might allow access with minimal prompts. However, if the attempt comes from an unfamiliar country or a previously unused device, the system can request additional verification steps. Adaptive authentication ensures that security measures are proportional to the risk, creating a balance between strong protection and user convenience.

Self-service capabilities also play a role in enhancing the user experience. Modern authentication platforms often include self-service options for tasks like password resets, account recovery, and access requests. By giving users more control over their accounts, organizations reduce the reliance on help desks and minimize downtime. Self-service tools empower users to resolve issues quickly, improving their satisfaction and productivity. Additionally, automated processes for onboarding and provisioning new accounts ensure that users can start working without unnecessary delays.

Cross-platform compatibility is another user-centric feature of modern authentication systems. With today's workforce and customer base accessing services from a mix of devices—ranging from desktops and laptops to smartphones, tablets, and IoT devices—authentication must be seamless across all platforms. Modern identity solutions provide consistent experiences, regardless of the device or operating system.

This continuity builds user confidence, encourages adoption of secure practices, and simplifies the overall authentication process.

User education and transparency further contribute to a better authentication experience. When users understand why certain security measures are in place and how they protect sensitive information, they are more likely to embrace modern authentication methods. Clear communication about the benefits of biometrics, the convenience of SSO, and the added protection of adaptive authentication fosters trust and reduces resistance to new technologies. By involving users in the transition to modern authentication, organizations can ensure smoother adoption and higher satisfaction.

For customers, a smooth authentication experience can directly impact brand loyalty and engagement. Lengthy or confusing login processes often lead to frustration, abandoned sessions, and lost business. Modern authentication solutions streamline customer onboarding, enable easy account recovery, and provide secure yet simple access to online services. By investing in user-friendly authentication, businesses improve their reputation, retain customers, and differentiate themselves in competitive markets.

Behind the scenes, modern authentication technologies also enable organizations to integrate advanced analytics and insights. Understanding how users interact with authentication processes—such as which methods they prefer, where they encounter difficulties, and how frequently they need help—allows companies to continually refine the experience. By monitoring user behavior and feedback, organizations can identify areas for improvement, implement targeted adjustments, and ultimately deliver a more intuitive and secure authentication journey.

Modern authentication not only strengthens security but also places users at the center of the experience. By leveraging biometrics, SSO, passwordless methods, adaptive authentication, and self-service tools, organizations create a seamless and efficient way for people to access their accounts and resources. These user-focused strategies increase satisfaction, boost productivity, and build trust, while also reducing the risks associated with traditional password-based systems. For businesses, adopting modern authentication approaches is a critical step toward delivering a more secure and enjoyable digital experience.

Identity Management in Multi-Cloud Scenarios

Managing identities in a multi-cloud environment presents unique challenges that require a thoughtful and strategic approach. As organizations increasingly adopt multiple cloud platforms—such as AWS, Microsoft Azure, and Google Cloud Platform—to take advantage of their respective strengths, they face the complex task of ensuring consistent, secure, and seamless identity management across these disparate systems. The ability to integrate identities, maintain uniform access controls, and enforce governance policies in a multi-cloud context is critical for both security and operational efficiency.

At the heart of multi-cloud identity management is the need for centralized control. Each cloud provider typically comes with its own native identity and access management (IAM) tools and conventions. For instance, AWS Identity and Access Management (IAM), Azure Active Directory, and Google Cloud IAM all provide robust features for managing roles, permissions, and authentication. However, these tools are generally designed to work best within their own ecosystems, which can lead to fragmentation when multiple platforms are in use. Without a unified strategy, organizations may struggle with inconsistent policies, duplicate user accounts, and increased administrative overhead.

A central identity provider or a federated identity model can help address these challenges. By integrating all cloud platforms with a common identity provider—whether on-premises Active Directory extended to the cloud, a dedicated cloud identity service, or a third-party federation solution—organizations can maintain a single source of truth for user identities. This approach ensures that users authenticate through one centralized system, with their access rights federated out to the individual cloud environments as needed. The result is a streamlined authentication process, consistent access controls, and a significant reduction in administrative complexity.

Federated identity frameworks rely on open standards such as SAML, OpenID Connect, and OAuth to establish trust between identity providers and cloud service providers. These standards facilitate secure token exchanges, allowing users to authenticate once and gain access to resources across multiple cloud platforms. With federation, administrators can define a single set of policies and then apply them uniformly, regardless of which cloud service the user is accessing. This consistency not only simplifies policy enforcement but also strengthens security by reducing the potential for configuration errors or policy mismatches.

Role-based access control (RBAC) and attribute-based access control (ABAC) play a crucial role in multi-cloud identity management. Defining roles and attributes centrally and then mapping them to the corresponding roles and policies in each cloud environment allows for granular control over user permissions. For example, a developer might be granted read-write access to development environments across all clouds but only read-only access to production resources. By enforcing these policies consistently, organizations can ensure that users have the appropriate level of access without over-provisioning privileges, thereby reducing the risk of accidental or malicious misuse.

Multi-cloud identity management also benefits from implementing single sign-on (SSO). SSO enables users to authenticate once and then access multiple cloud platforms without re-entering their credentials. This improves the user experience by reducing login friction and password fatigue, while also enhancing security by centralizing authentication. When combined with multi-factor authentication (MFA), SSO ensures that all access points—across every cloud platform—are protected with a strong layer of security. By integrating SSO solutions that support multiple cloud providers, organizations can maintain a consistent user experience while bolstering security across their entire cloud ecosystem.

Automation and orchestration are key to scaling identity management in multi-cloud scenarios. As organizations grow, the number of users, roles, and resources increases exponentially. Automating user provisioning, access reviews, and policy enforcement ensures that identity processes remain efficient and accurate. Automation tools can also help synchronize identities and roles between on-premises directories and cloud platforms, reducing the risk of human error and ensuring that users always have the correct access. Furthermore, orchestration platforms can manage identity workflows across multiple clouds, making it easier to onboard new employees, provision resources, and maintain compliance.

Compliance and regulatory requirements add another layer of complexity to multi-cloud identity management. Many industries must adhere to strict data protection laws and security standards that mandate detailed access controls, auditing, and reporting. Maintaining compliance in a multi-cloud environment requires a unified approach to monitoring and logging identity-related activities. Centralized reporting tools can consolidate audit logs from all cloud platforms, providing a single view of who accessed what, when, and under what conditions. This visibility is critical for demonstrating compliance, identifying potential security incidents, and responding quickly to threats.

Zero Trust principles further enhance security in multi-cloud scenarios. In a Zero Trust model, no user or device is inherently trusted, regardless of whether they are inside or outside the network perimeter. Every access request is continuously verified, and the least-privilege principle is enforced. Multi-cloud identity management that embraces Zero Trust ensures that users are granted only the permissions they need, for the shortest amount of time required, and that every action is logged and analyzed for potential threats. By integrating Zero Trust practices into multi-cloud identity strategies, organizations can better protect sensitive data and prevent unauthorized access.

As organizations continue to expand their use of multiple cloud platforms, the importance of a cohesive identity management strategy cannot be overstated. By centralizing identities, standardizing policies, and leveraging advanced automation and security techniques, businesses can achieve a secure, scalable, and user-friendly identity framework that spans their entire multi-cloud environment. This approach not only simplifies administration but also strengthens security, enhances user productivity, and ensures compliance with industry regulations.

Compliance Requirements and Identity Management

Compliance requirements have become a driving force behind modern identity management practices. As data breaches and cybersecurity threats continue to rise, governments and regulatory bodies have established stringent standards to protect sensitive information and ensure secure access to critical systems. Identity management serves as a cornerstone for meeting these requirements, providing organizations with the tools and processes necessary to enforce access controls, maintain audit trails, and demonstrate accountability. By aligning identity management strategies with compliance mandates, businesses can safeguard their digital assets, build trust with customers, and avoid costly fines or legal repercussions.

One of the primary compliance standards that influence identity management is the General Data Protection Regulation (GDPR). GDPR sets strict rules for handling personal data, including the need to restrict access to only those who require it and to keep detailed records of who accessed what information and when. Identity management solutions play a vital role in fulfilling these requirements by enforcing the principle of least privilege, ensuring that users only have access to the data necessary for their roles. By implementing strong identity governance frameworks, organizations can control access more effectively, prevent unauthorized access, and maintain the detailed logs needed for GDPR compliance.

Similarly, the Health Insurance Portability and Accountability Act (HIPAA) places significant demands on identity management in the healthcare sector. HIPAA mandates that organizations handling protected health information (PHI) implement robust access controls and ensure that only authorized personnel can view sensitive medical records. Identity management systems provide role-based access controls, automated provisioning and deprovisioning, and advanced authentication measures to meet these requirements. By integrating multi-factor authentication (MFA) and continuous access monitoring, healthcare organizations can enhance security and reduce the risk of unauthorized access, thereby maintaining compliance with HIPAA's strict security rules.

The Payment Card Industry Data Security Standard (PCI DSS) also relies heavily on identity management. PCI DSS requires organizations that process credit card transactions to maintain strict controls over user access to cardholder data environments. This includes limiting administrative privileges, regularly reviewing access rights, and ensuring that all accounts have unique credentials. Identity management solutions automate many of these processes, making it easier for businesses to stay compliant. By providing detailed reporting and audit trails, these systems allow organizations to demonstrate compliance during audits and quickly address any identified vulnerabilities.

In addition to industry-specific standards, many countries have implemented their own cybersecurity regulations. For example, the Cybersecurity Maturity Model Certification (CMMC) in the United States and the Network and Information Security (NIS) Directive in the European Union require organizations to implement robust identity and access controls as part of their overall security frameworks. Identity management solutions help organizations comply with these regulations by standardizing access policies, centralizing user directories, and maintaining clear records of all identity-related activities. By using identity management as a foundation, businesses can more easily meet the diverse compliance requirements of different regions and industries.

Auditing and reporting are integral to compliance efforts, and identity management systems excel in providing the transparency needed for regulatory audits. These systems generate detailed logs of user activity, including login attempts, changes to permissions, and access to sensitive data. When auditors or regulators request evidence of compliance, organizations can produce comprehensive reports that demonstrate their adherence to security policies. These reports not only show that the organization is following best practices but also help identify areas for improvement, enabling a more proactive approach to maintaining compliance over time.

Identity governance and administration (IGA) tools further enhance compliance by automating key processes such as access certification and role reviews. Compliance standards often require periodic verification that users still need their assigned privileges. IGA tools streamline this process by presenting managers with clear, actionable reports that show who has access to what resources. If a user no longer requires certain permissions, these tools make it easy to revoke access promptly. By automating access reviews and certifications, organizations can maintain continuous compliance and reduce the administrative burden on IT teams.

Another critical aspect of compliance is the ability to respond quickly to security incidents. When a breach occurs, regulators often require organizations to provide a detailed account of what happened, who was involved, and what measures were taken to mitigate the damage. Identity management systems provide the visibility needed to meet these demands. With centralized logging and real-time monitoring, organizations can trace the steps of an attacker, determine how they gained access, and identify which data was compromised. This level of insight not only supports compliance investigations but also helps organizations strengthen their defenses against future incidents.

Modern identity management platforms also incorporate advanced security features that align with compliance requirements. For example, adaptive authentication and risk-based access controls ensure that high-risk login attempts are subject to additional verification, while low-risk access is granted seamlessly. These intelligent security measures help organizations maintain compliance by enforcing stronger authentication protocols without creating unnecessary friction for legitimate users. By integrating these features into their identity management strategies, businesses can stay ahead of regulatory requirements and demonstrate their commitment to protecting sensitive data.

As compliance requirements continue to evolve, identity management will remain a critical component of any organization's security strategy. By leveraging robust identity governance frameworks, advanced authentication methods, and automated processes, businesses can maintain a secure and compliant environment. In turn, this fosters trust with customers, partners, and regulators while reducing the risk of financial penalties and reputational damage. By staying proactive and investing in modern identity management solutions, organizations can navigate the complex landscape of compliance with confidence and efficiency.

Cloud Identity in the DevOps Workflow

Cloud identity management has become a vital part of the DevOps workflow as organizations increasingly rely on automated pipelines and distributed teams to accelerate software delivery. In the fast-paced world of DevOps, secure and efficient access to resources is essential. Engineers, developers, testers, and operations staff need seamless yet controlled access to code repositories, build servers, cloud environments, and deployment tools. Without proper identity management, maintaining security and compliance across these touchpoints becomes nearly impossible. A robust cloud identity strategy ensures that every individual and system in the DevOps lifecycle is properly authenticated, authorized, and monitored, supporting both speed and security.

One of the primary challenges in the DevOps workflow is ensuring that only authorized users and systems can interact with the various tools and services used in the development lifecycle. Developers often need access to source code repositories, CI/CD (Continuous Integration/Continuous Deployment) platforms, artifact registries, and cloud environments. Meanwhile, automated systems and service accounts also require permissions to run builds, execute tests, and deploy applications. Cloud identity solutions provide a centralized way to manage these credentials and ensure that only the right people or systems can perform these actions. By leveraging identity providers, organizations can streamline authentication and reduce the risk of credentials being shared or stored insecurely.

Centralized identity management also simplifies the process of granting and revoking access. In a DevOps environment, team members may change roles frequently, and external contractors or third-party vendors may come and go. Having a unified identity platform allows administrators to quickly adjust permissions and ensure that only current, authorized users have access. This agility is especially important in fast-moving development cycles, where delays in provisioning or deprovisioning access can slow down deployments or introduce security vulnerabilities.

Role-based access control (RBAC) and attribute-based access control (ABAC) are particularly useful in the DevOps workflow. RBAC assigns permissions based on roles, such as "developer," "tester," or "build engineer," ensuring that individuals only have the access they need to perform their duties. ABAC takes this a step further by adding contextual attributes like time of day, project status, or device type. For example, a developer might only be allowed to deploy code during certain stages of the pipeline or from a trusted corporate device. By using these access control models, organizations can enforce the principle of least privilege and significantly reduce their attack surface.

Secrets management is another critical aspect of cloud identity in the DevOps workflow. Secrets such as API keys, tokens, SSH keys, and passwords are often required to integrate tools, access cloud resources, or deploy applications. Managing these secrets manually or storing them in plain text increases the risk of accidental exposure. Modern identity solutions integrate with secrets management tools that securely store and rotate credentials. By tying these secrets to centralized identity providers, organizations can enforce policies that ensure credentials are only available to authenticated and authorized users or systems. This approach not only enhances security but also simplifies compliance efforts.

Multi-factor authentication (MFA) is another layer of protection that strengthens identity management in DevOps. While automated systems may rely on machine-to-machine authentication, human users accessing the pipeline, production environments, or cloud consoles can benefit from MFA. Requiring a second factor—such as a time-based one-time password (TOTP) or a hardware security key—helps ensure that even if primary credentials are compromised, unauthorized access is prevented. Many cloud identity providers support MFA natively, making it straightforward to enforce this additional security step without disrupting the development workflow.

Auditing and monitoring capabilities are essential to maintaining a secure and compliant DevOps pipeline. Cloud identity platforms provide detailed logs of authentication events, access requests, and policy changes. These logs allow security teams to trace the origin of any suspicious activity and ensure that only authorized users are performing critical actions like deploying to production or modifying infrastructure configurations. Real-time monitoring and alerting further enhance visibility, enabling organizations to detect and respond to potential threats before they cause damage.

Cloud identity solutions also enable smooth integrations with CI/CD pipelines. Many modern CI/CD platforms support integration with popular identity providers, allowing developers and build agents to authenticate securely without managing credentials directly. This integration not only streamlines the build and deployment process but also ensures that every step in the pipeline is securely authenticated. As a result, organizations can maintain the rapid pace of DevOps while still adhering to strict security and compliance standards.

The adoption of a cloud-native approach has further elevated the importance of identity management in the DevOps workflow. Containers, microservices, and serverless architectures rely heavily on APIs, service accounts, and automated processes. In these environments, traditional perimeter-based security models no longer apply. Instead, identity becomes the foundation of security. By verifying every user, process, and service before granting access, organizations can ensure that their DevOps pipelines remain secure even as their infrastructure scales and evolves.

Cloud identity management in the DevOps workflow also supports Zero Trust principles. Zero Trust shifts the security paradigm from trusting users and systems based on their location to continuously verifying their identity and context. In a DevOps environment, this means that every code commit, every build job, and every deployment step is authenticated and authorized in real time. By adopting a Zero Trust approach, organizations can reduce the risk of insider threats, ensure consistent enforcement of access policies, and maintain a high level of security even in highly dynamic and distributed environments.

Ultimately, cloud identity in the DevOps workflow is not just a technical necessity but a strategic enabler. By centralizing identity management, enforcing strong access controls, integrating with CI/CD platforms, and embracing advanced security measures like MFA and Zero Trust, organizations can ensure that their development pipelines remain secure, efficient, and compliant. As DevOps practices continue to evolve, a robust cloud identity strategy will remain a critical component of successful and secure software delivery.

Identity Automation and Workflow Management

Identity automation and workflow management have become crucial components of modern identity and access management (IAM) strategies. As organizations expand their digital ecosystems and embrace cloud technologies, managing user identities, permissions, and access requests manually is no longer feasible. Automated identity solutions streamline these processes by reducing the need for human intervention, improving accuracy, and increasing efficiency. At the same time, well-defined workflows ensure that identity-related tasks follow a consistent, repeatable pattern, helping maintain compliance, improve security, and enhance the overall user experience.

Automation begins with the identity lifecycle. This lifecycle includes provisioning new accounts, updating access rights as roles change, and deprovisioning accounts when employees leave the organization. Automating these tasks ensures that users have the appropriate access levels at all times. For example, when a new employee is onboarded, an automated identity system can instantly provision their accounts across multiple platforms, assign the necessary roles and permissions, and send out any required credentials. This reduces delays, improves productivity, and decreases the risk of errors that might lead to security vulnerabilities or compliance issues.

Role-based access control (RBAC) and attribute-based access control (ABAC) are integral to identity automation. By defining roles and attributes in advance, organizations can apply policies automatically when new users or systems are added. A user assigned to a particular department or job function can automatically receive the correct level of access without the need for manual intervention. These policies can also be updated dynamically, so if a user's responsibilities change, their access can be adjusted in real time. This ensures that permissions are always in sync with current business needs, reducing the risk of over-privileged accounts and potential insider threats.

Self-service capabilities are another significant advantage of automated identity workflows. Allowing users to request additional access, reset their passwords, or manage their profile information through a self-service portal reduces the burden on IT staff. Instead of waiting for manual approval, users can submit requests that are routed through predefined workflows. For instance, an access request might automatically be forwarded to a manager for approval and then to a compliance officer for review, all without human intervention. Once the necessary approvals are in place, the system can automatically grant the requested access. This streamlined process improves response times, enhances user satisfaction, and allows IT teams to focus on more strategic initiatives.

Integrating identity automation with other enterprise systems further enhances its value. By connecting IAM solutions to human resources (HR) platforms, organizations can trigger identity workflows based on HR events. When an employee is hired, promoted, or leaves the company, the IAM system can respond automatically. For example, a new hire event in the HR system could initiate a workflow that provisions email accounts, grants access to project management tools, and enrolls the employee in mandatory training courses. Similarly, when an employee's departure is recorded, the workflow could immediately deactivate their accounts, revoke access rights, and archive relevant data. This integration ensures that identity processes are always aligned with organizational changes, improving both security and operational efficiency.

Automation also plays a critical role in maintaining compliance. Many regulatory frameworks, such as GDPR, HIPAA, and SOX, require organizations to enforce strict access controls and keep detailed records of user activity. Automated workflows help ensure that these controls are consistently applied. They can also generate audit trails that demonstrate compliance. For example, when a user is granted access to a restricted system, the workflow can automatically log the approval process, note who authorized the access, and record the time and date of the change. These logs provide transparency and accountability, making it easier to pass audits and identify potential security risks.

Another important aspect of identity automation is the ability to handle large-scale events, such as company mergers, acquisitions, or rapid growth. In these scenarios, the number of user accounts and access requests can increase dramatically. Automating identity processes enables organizations to scale quickly without compromising security or efficiency. Instead of manually provisioning thousands of accounts, the IAM system can apply standardized workflows that ensure consistent policies, reduce errors, and speed up the entire process. This scalability is particularly valuable for global organizations that manage identities across multiple regions, time zones, and regulatory environments.

Workflow management also enhances security by ensuring that identity-related tasks follow established guidelines and approval chains. Each step in a workflow can be designed to include built-in checks and balances. For instance, when a privileged account is created or updated, the workflow might require multiple levels of approval before granting the requested permissions. This reduces the risk of unauthorized access, helps prevent insider threats, and ensures that all changes are carefully reviewed before implementation. By embedding security into every step of the process, automated workflows help maintain a strong, resilient IAM program.

As technology continues to evolve, identity automation and workflow management are likely to incorporate more advanced capabilities.

Machine learning and artificial intelligence can help identify patterns, detect anomalies, and recommend workflow optimizations. For example, AI might analyze historical access requests and suggest more efficient approval paths or flag unusual behavior that could indicate a security threat. These intelligent features not only improve efficiency but also enhance security by identifying and responding to risks in real time.

Identity automation and workflow management have become essential for organizations seeking to streamline their IAM processes, improve security, and maintain compliance. By automating repetitive tasks, integrating with other enterprise systems, and enforcing consistent workflows, businesses can create a more efficient, secure, and user-friendly identity environment. This approach not only reduces administrative overhead but also helps organizations scale their identity practices and adapt to a rapidly changing digital landscape.

Zero Trust Principles and Cloud Identity

Zero Trust has become a cornerstone of modern cybersecurity, reshaping the way organizations think about access control, data protection, and identity management. Unlike traditional perimeter-based security models, Zero Trust operates on the principle that no user, device, or system is inherently trusted—regardless of whether it resides inside or outside the network perimeter. Instead, trust must be continually earned, verified, and re-verified based on a combination of context, behavior, and risk. When integrated with cloud identity solutions, Zero Trust principles provide a scalable, adaptable framework for securing resources, managing access, and mitigating modern cyber threats.

At the core of Zero Trust is the idea that identity is the new perimeter. In a cloud-first world where applications, data, and users frequently exist beyond traditional network boundaries, the identity of a user or system becomes the most reliable way to establish trust. Rather than relying on the physical location of a device or the network segment it resides on, Zero Trust places identity at the center of all security decisions. This shift allows organizations to secure their environments regardless of how distributed their infrastructure or workforce may be.

One of the foundational principles of Zero Trust is "never trust, always verify." This means that every access request, regardless of its origin, is subject to continuous verification. Instead of granting broad, implicit access based on network location, Zero Trust requires that each request be authenticated, authorized, and evaluated against dynamic policies. Cloud identity platforms enable this approach by providing centralized identity stores, real-time authentication, and advanced policy enforcement mechanisms. By integrating these capabilities, organizations can ensure that only legitimate, verified identities can access sensitive resources.

Least privilege access is another key principle of Zero Trust, emphasizing that users and systems should only have the minimal level of access required to perform their tasks. This principle reduces the attack surface, limits the potential damage from compromised accounts, and helps prevent unauthorized lateral movement within the environment. Cloud identity solutions help enforce least privilege by providing fine-grained access controls, role-based access control (RBAC), and attribute-based access control (ABAC). With these tools, organizations can define and apply precise policies that align with Zero Trust principles, ensuring that access is only granted when absolutely necessary.

Continuous monitoring and risk assessment are central to Zero Trust. Since trust is never permanent, Zero Trust frameworks rely on ongoing evaluations of user behavior, device health, and contextual signals. For example, if a user typically logs in from a corporate office but suddenly attempts to access resources from an unfamiliar country, the system may require additional verification steps. Similarly, if a device fails to meet security standards—such as running outdated software or lacking endpoint protection—it may be restricted from accessing certain resources. Cloud identity providers often integrate risk-based authentication and adaptive policies, enabling organizations to dynamically adjust access requirements based on real-time risk assessments.

Multi-factor authentication (MFA) is a critical component of Zero Trust, providing an additional layer of verification for all users. MFA ensures that even if primary credentials are compromised, unauthorized access can be prevented by requiring a second factor—such as a push notification, biometric scan, or security key. Cloud identity solutions make implementing MFA straightforward and scalable, allowing organizations to enforce strong authentication requirements without adding unnecessary complexity. By integrating MFA into a Zero Trust strategy, businesses can enhance security while still providing a seamless experience for users.

Cloud identity platforms also support the Zero Trust principle of segmentation. Instead of treating the entire network as a single trusted zone, segmentation involves dividing resources into smaller, more manageable units. Each segment can have its own access controls, policies, and security requirements. This approach limits the impact of potential breaches and makes it easier to enforce granular security measures. Cloud identity solutions help enforce segmentation by applying policies at the identity level, ensuring that access to each segment is tightly controlled and continuously monitored.

Automation and orchestration play a crucial role in Zero Trust frameworks. As environments become more complex, manual processes are no longer sufficient to maintain security and compliance. Cloud identity solutions can automate many aspects of identity lifecycle management, from provisioning and deprovisioning accounts to updating access policies based on user roles or behavioral changes. This automation ensures that security policies remain up-to-date and consistently applied, reducing human error and improving overall security posture.

Zero Trust principles also align closely with compliance requirements and regulatory standards. Many frameworks—such as GDPR, HIPAA, and SOC 2—emphasize strict access controls, continuous monitoring, and detailed auditing. By implementing Zero Trust with cloud identity solutions, organizations can more easily meet these compliance obligations. Cloud identity platforms provide centralized logging, real-time policy enforcement, and automated reporting capabilities, making it simpler to demonstrate compliance and respond to audits.

Zero Trust is not a single product or technology; it is a comprehensive strategy that encompasses identity, access control, and continuous monitoring. Cloud identity solutions serve as the foundation for implementing Zero Trust principles, providing the tools and infrastructure needed to establish, verify, and maintain trust at every level. As cyber threats continue to evolve, embracing Zero Trust with a strong focus on cloud identity will help organizations stay ahead of attackers, protect their resources, and adapt to the challenges of an increasingly complex digital landscape.

Auditing and Monitoring Identity Activity

Auditing and monitoring identity activity have become fundamental practices in ensuring the security, compliance, and operational efficiency of an organization's identity and access management (IAM) framework. With the rise of sophisticated cyber threats, regulatory requirements, and increasingly complex IT environments, organizations need visibility into how identities are used, how access is granted, and how resources are being utilized. By implementing comprehensive auditing and monitoring processes, organizations can detect anomalies, prevent unauthorized access, and maintain a high level of accountability across their systems.

Auditing involves the systematic recording and review of all identity-related actions within an IT environment. These actions may include user authentications, privilege escalations, password changes, role assignments, and account deactivations. The goal of auditing is to create an immutable trail of events that can be examined forensically when needed. This historical record helps organizations understand how and when changes occurred, who made them, and whether they aligned with established policies. In addition to strengthening security, this detailed documentation is often required by industry regulations such as GDPR, HIPAA, and PCI DSS.

Monitoring, on the other hand, involves the continuous, real-time observation of identity activities. While auditing looks at past actions, monitoring provides insight into what is happening right now. This enables organizations to detect suspicious behaviors as they occur, allowing for immediate response. For example, if a user account that typically logs in during business hours suddenly attempts to access resources in the middle of the night from a foreign IP address, monitoring tools can flag this activity. Security teams can then investigate further, apply additional authentication requirements, or temporarily lock the account until the anomaly is resolved.

Combining auditing and monitoring creates a comprehensive approach to identity security. Auditing ensures that there is a reliable record of all identity-related events, providing transparency and accountability. Monitoring, meanwhile, offers the ability to respond to threats in real time, reducing the window of opportunity for attackers. Together, these practices form a robust defense against insider threats, credential misuse, and external attacks.

Centralized logging is a key component of effective auditing and monitoring. By consolidating identity activity logs from multiple sources—such as directory services, cloud identity providers, single sign-on platforms, and privilege management solutions—organizations gain a single, unified view of all identity-related events. This centralization simplifies the process of searching, filtering, and analyzing logs, making it easier to spot patterns, detect anomalies, and produce detailed reports. Centralized logging also streamlines compliance efforts by ensuring that auditors can quickly access the data they need.

Advanced analytics further enhance auditing and monitoring capabilities. Modern IAM solutions often incorporate machine learning and artificial intelligence to identify subtle patterns that might be missed by traditional methods. By analyzing historical data and applying algorithms, these systems can predict which activities are likely normal and which might indicate a security threat. For instance, if an employee's account suddenly requests access to a sensitive database they've never used before, the analytics engine can flag the activity as unusual and escalate it for review. This proactive approach helps organizations stay ahead of evolving threats and respond more effectively.

Another critical aspect of identity activity auditing and monitoring is privileged access management (PAM). Privileged accounts—those with administrative rights or elevated permissions—pose a particularly high risk if compromised. Auditing privileged actions ensures that every administrative change is recorded and traceable, while monitoring privileged sessions in real time provides an added layer of oversight. With tools like session recording, organizations can review exactly what actions were taken by privileged users and ensure that they align with security policies. If a privileged user attempts to disable logging or create unauthorized backdoor accounts, real-time monitoring can detect and alert security teams immediately.

Regulatory compliance is a major driver behind auditing and monitoring efforts. Industry regulations and standards often require detailed records of who accessed what and when, as well as evidence that access controls are functioning properly. Auditing provides the documentation needed to demonstrate compliance, while monitoring ensures that violations are detected and addressed promptly. By maintaining a thorough record of identity activity and continuously observing user behavior, organizations can meet their compliance obligations, avoid penalties, and maintain trust with customers and stakeholders.

Auditing and monitoring also contribute to continuous improvement in identity and access management. By reviewing audit logs and monitoring data, organizations can identify patterns and trends that reveal weaknesses in their IAM policies. For example, frequent failed login attempts might indicate overly complex password policies or a lack of proper user training. Reviewing access requests and approvals might uncover instances where roles and permissions are not clearly defined. With these insights, organizations can refine their IAM processes, strengthen their security posture, and enhance the user experience.

Implementing a comprehensive auditing and monitoring strategy requires the right tools and technologies. Many IAM platforms include built-in auditing and monitoring features, while others can integrate with third-party security information and event management (SIEM) solutions. SIEM tools aggregate and analyze identity activity logs, provide real-time alerts, and generate detailed compliance reports.

Additionally, organizations can deploy specialized analytics platforms that use machine learning to detect anomalies, correlate events, and predict potential risks. By leveraging these technologies, organizations can create a robust and scalable framework for auditing and monitoring identity activity.

Auditing and monitoring identity activity are no longer optional in today's threat landscape. These practices provide the visibility, accountability, and proactive defense mechanisms needed to protect sensitive resources, meet regulatory requirements, and maintain trust. By centralizing logs, applying advanced analytics, and continuously observing user behavior, organizations can stay one step ahead of cyber threats and ensure that their identity and access management programs remain effective and resilient.

Managing External Identities and B2B Access

As organizations expand their operations and collaborate with a growing network of partners, vendors, contractors, and external customers, managing external identities and B2B access becomes a critical aspect of their identity and access management (IAM) strategy. Unlike internal users, whose identities are typically managed within a single corporate directory, external users come from a wide variety of sources and may not conform to the same identity management policies. The challenge lies in granting these external users secure, seamless access to specific resources while maintaining strict controls, ensuring compliance, and minimizing administrative overhead.

One of the first considerations in managing external identities is determining how these identities are represented and stored. In many cases, external users are not directly enrolled into the organization's primary directory. Instead, organizations may rely on federated identity models, where external identities are managed by the users' own organizations and then linked to the host organization's environment through standardized protocols. This approach allows external users to authenticate with their existing credentials, which reduces complexity for both parties. Standards such as SAML, OpenID Connect, and OAuth enable these federations, ensuring that identity assertions can be securely shared and verified without transferring credentials.

When federation is not possible—perhaps because some external users do not have a corporate identity provider—organizations can adopt a multi-directory or multi-tenant model. In this approach, external identities are stored in a separate directory service specifically for partners, vendors, and other third parties. This segmentation ensures that external accounts are clearly distinguished from internal accounts, making it easier to apply unique access policies, implement tighter security controls, and maintain accurate auditing. By isolating external identities, organizations also reduce the risk of external user accounts accidentally gaining access to internal systems or sensitive data.

Access management for external users often requires more granular control than what is applied to internal employees. Unlike internal staff, external users typically need access to only a subset of the organization's resources. This makes role-based access control (RBAC) and attribute-based access control (ABAC) essential tools for managing external identities. Organizations can define roles that match common external use cases—such as "partner vendor" or "contractor"—and assign permissions that limit access to only the necessary applications, files, or data sets. By leveraging attributes, such as project assignment, geographical location, or contract expiration date, organizations can further refine access policies. This ensures that external users only have access for as long as they need it, and only to what they need to perform their roles.

Another critical component of managing external identities is the onboarding and offboarding process. External users often have shorter engagement cycles than full-time employees, which means the identity lifecycle must be efficient and well-structured. Automating the onboarding process ensures that new external users receive the correct access quickly, without requiring time-consuming manual interventions. Self-service portals can further simplify onboarding by allowing external users to register themselves, providing the necessary verification documents, and selecting their appropriate roles. This streamlined process improves the experience for external users while reducing administrative workload.

Offboarding external users is equally important. When a contract ends or a partner's involvement with a project concludes, their access must be revoked promptly to prevent any potential security risks. Automated offboarding workflows ensure that all associated accounts, permissions, and credentials are disabled or removed. This not only reduces the risk of unauthorized access but also maintains a clean, well-organized identity environment. Automated deprovisioning also helps with compliance by ensuring that no external accounts linger with active permissions beyond their intended lifespan.

Security is a paramount concern when managing external identities. External users may access resources from different networks, devices, or geographic locations, increasing the risk of account compromise. Multi-factor authentication (MFA) is a critical security measure for verifying external users' identities, even if their credentials have been compromised. Additionally, adaptive authentication can be employed to enforce stricter controls under certain conditions—such as when external users access sensitive systems or when login attempts come from unrecognized devices or IP addresses. By implementing these measures, organizations can significantly reduce the likelihood of unauthorized access or data breaches.

Compliance requirements also play a significant role in shaping external identity management policies. Regulations such as GDPR, CCPA, and industry-specific standards often require organizations to maintain detailed records of who accessed sensitive data and when. Ensuring that external identities are subject to the same level of auditability as internal identities is crucial. Identity management platforms with robust logging and reporting capabilities provide the transparency needed to demonstrate compliance. By maintaining comprehensive logs, organizations can easily track external user activity, review access requests, and provide evidence during audits.

Another consideration is the user experience for external users. A cumbersome authentication or access process can frustrate partners, vendors, and customers, potentially harming business relationships.

Streamlining the authentication process, enabling single sign-on (SSO) for external users, and providing self-service password reset capabilities improve the overall experience. A positive user experience not only increases satisfaction but also reduces the likelihood that users will bypass security measures or engage in risky behaviors.

As organizations rely more heavily on external collaborators, contractors, and partners, managing external identities and B2B access will continue to grow in importance. By employing federation standards, implementing robust RBAC and ABAC policies, automating lifecycle management, and applying advanced security measures, organizations can ensure that external users can access the resources they need while maintaining strong security controls and compliance. This approach not only protects sensitive data but also enables seamless collaboration, helping organizations thrive in an interconnected business environment.

Secure Collaboration with Cloud Identities

As businesses expand their use of cloud-based tools and services, secure collaboration becomes an essential part of maintaining productivity and protecting sensitive information. The widespread adoption of cloud platforms, combined with a growing reliance on external partners and remote workforces, has fundamentally changed how organizations approach identity management. Cloud identities serve as the foundation for enabling secure collaboration across distributed teams, external contractors, and third-party vendors. By integrating identity solutions that emphasize security, transparency, and ease of use, companies can foster efficient, secure collaboration while mitigating risks.

Cloud identities provide a centralized approach to managing users, devices, and access rights. This centralized structure is especially valuable in collaborative scenarios where multiple parties need access to shared resources. For example, a marketing agency might work with external contractors, advertising partners, and design freelancers. By using cloud-based identity services, the agency can grant these external collaborators appropriate access to files, messaging platforms, and project management tools without creating multiple, disparate accounts or relying on insecure workarounds. Centralized identity management ensures that all participants have the right level of access, and that access can be adjusted or revoked quickly as projects evolve.

One of the most significant advantages of cloud identities in secure collaboration is the ability to enforce consistent security policies across all users and devices. Whether an employee is working from an office, a remote location, or on a mobile device, the same access controls and authentication requirements apply. This consistency reduces the risk of configuration errors and helps ensure that all collaborators adhere to the organization's security standards. By using a single identity provider or federated identity model, companies can maintain strict control over authentication methods, password policies, and multi-factor authentication (MFA) requirements, regardless of where users are located or which devices they use.

Federated identity solutions further enhance secure collaboration by enabling trust relationships between organizations. In many collaborative efforts, multiple companies work together on shared projects, each with its own identity management system. Instead of creating new accounts for every external user, federated identity models allow users to authenticate using their existing corporate credentials. This approach simplifies the onboarding process, reduces the need for managing multiple sets of credentials, and ensures that external users are subject to their own organization's security policies. As a result, companies can build seamless and secure collaboration environments without increasing administrative overhead or compromising security.

Single sign-on (SSO) is another key feature that supports secure collaboration. SSO allows users to log in once and gain access to multiple applications and services without having to re-enter their credentials. In a collaborative environment, this means that participants can move seamlessly between shared file repositories, communication tools, and cloud-based productivity suites. Not only does this improve the user experience, but it also enhances security by reducing the number of credentials that need to be managed and stored. With SSO, organizations can maintain a more streamlined authentication process and ensure that all collaborators use secure, centralized login methods.

Access control is a critical component of secure collaboration. While cloud identities provide a unified way to authenticate users, it is equally important to control what users can do once they are logged in. Role-based access control (RBAC) and attribute-based access control (ABAC) allow administrators to define fine-grained permissions based on user roles, responsibilities, and contextual attributes. For instance, a financial analyst might have read-only access to budget reports, while a project manager could have edit permissions for the same files. By applying these controls, companies can ensure that collaborators only have access to the data and tools they need, reducing the risk of data leaks and unauthorized actions.

Collaboration often involves sharing resources beyond the immediate organizational boundary, which introduces unique security challenges. Cloud identities help address these challenges by providing detailed auditing and monitoring capabilities. Every authentication attempt, file access, and privilege change is logged, creating a comprehensive record of all collaborative activities. Security teams can analyze these logs to detect suspicious behavior, such as repeated failed login attempts, unexpected access patterns, or unauthorized privilege escalations. By continuously monitoring identity-related activities, organizations can respond quickly to potential threats and maintain a secure collaboration environment.

Another important aspect of secure collaboration is data governance and compliance. Many industries require strict adherence to regulatory standards for handling sensitive information. Cloud identity platforms simplify compliance by ensuring that all access is authenticated, authorized, and documented. Automated workflows for granting and revoking access, along with detailed reporting, provide the transparency needed to demonstrate compliance during audits. This capability is particularly important in highly regulated sectors such as healthcare, finance, and government, where secure collaboration must align with rigorous data protection requirements.

User experience also plays a vital role in secure collaboration. A frictionless identity solution encourages participants to follow best practices rather than seeking workarounds. For example, if a secure, user-friendly single sign-on portal is available, collaborators are less likely to rely on insecure methods like sharing passwords or emailing sensitive files. By combining robust security measures with a streamlined user experience, organizations can ensure that secure collaboration is not only effective but also convenient.

Cloud identities enable organizations to strike the right balance between security and accessibility, making it easier to collaborate across teams, companies, and geographical boundaries. Through centralized management, consistent policies, federation, SSO, and detailed monitoring, businesses can create secure environments that foster trust and efficiency. As the reliance on cloud-based collaboration continues to grow, the importance of cloud identities in maintaining a secure and productive digital workplace will only increase.

Identity Management for Mobile and IoT Devices

The proliferation of mobile devices and Internet of Things (IoT) endpoints has significantly expanded the attack surface for organizations. Smartphones, tablets, smart watches, connected sensors, industrial machinery, and even medical devices now routinely connect to enterprise networks and access sensitive resources. Each of these devices represents an identity that must be secured, managed, and monitored to prevent unauthorized access, maintain compliance, and ensure operational stability. As mobile and IoT adoption continues to grow, identity management strategies must evolve to address the unique challenges posed by these devices.

Mobile devices have become integral to the modern workplace. Employees rely on smartphones and tablets not only for communication but also for accessing corporate applications, files, and data while on the go. However, these devices are often outside the organization's direct control, making them more vulnerable to compromise. Unlike traditional endpoints like desktop PCs, mobile devices frequently connect to unsecured Wi-Fi networks, are carried into various physical locations, and may be used for both personal and business purposes. This creates a need for identity management solutions that can handle device variability, unpredictable usage patterns, and the potential for frequent ownership changes.

IoT devices add another layer of complexity. While mobile devices are typically user-driven, IoT endpoints are often autonomous, continuously collecting, transmitting, or processing data. These devices can range from simple environmental sensors to complex industrial control systems, each with its own identity and set of permissions. Many IoT devices are not designed with robust security in mind, lacking the built-in authentication and encryption mechanisms found in more traditional endpoints. Identity management for IoT must address these inherent limitations by implementing strong authentication, securing communication channels, and ensuring that each device's identity is verifiable.

A critical aspect of managing mobile and IoT identities is device enrollment. Before granting access to corporate resources, each device must be registered and verified. For mobile devices, this often involves an onboarding process where users authenticate themselves and then enroll their device into a mobile device management (MDM) or enterprise mobility management (EMM) platform. The platform assigns a unique identifier to the device, links it to the user's corporate identity, and applies the appropriate security policies. IoT devices, on the other hand, may be enrolled through a provisioning process that involves factory-installed credentials, digital certificates, or secure tokens. Once enrolled, these devices are continuously monitored to ensure compliance with organizational policies.

Authentication plays a central role in securing mobile and IoT identities. Multi-factor authentication (MFA) is a standard practice for mobile devices, combining something the user knows (like a password) with something they have (such as a mobile authenticator app or hardware token). Biometric authentication methods—such as fingerprint scanning or facial recognition—further enhance security by adding a layer of verification that is unique to the user. IoT devices, however, often require different approaches. Because they lack traditional user interfaces, authentication may rely on device certificates, secure tokens, or cryptographic keys embedded in the hardware. Ensuring that every device—whether mobile or IoT—is authenticated before accessing the network helps prevent unauthorized access and reduces the risk of data breaches.

Once authenticated, devices must be continuously monitored and managed. Identity management platforms provide centralized dashboards that allow administrators to track device status, review access logs, and enforce security policies. For example, if a mobile device is lost or stolen, administrators can immediately revoke its access, remotely wipe its data, or block it from connecting to sensitive resources. Similarly, if an IoT device begins to behave abnormally— such as sending unexpected traffic or failing to authenticate—security teams can quickly identify the issue, investigate its cause, and take corrective action. This real-time visibility into device activity is essential for maintaining a secure environment.

Another challenge in managing mobile and IoT identities is the need for scalable, automated processes. As the number of connected devices grows, manual provisioning and deprovisioning become impractical. Automated workflows ensure that new devices are quickly assigned the correct permissions and that old or compromised devices are removed from the network without delay. For IoT environments in particular, where thousands or even millions of endpoints may be deployed, automation is critical to maintaining consistent security policies and minimizing human error.

Compliance requirements further highlight the importance of robust identity management for mobile and IoT devices. Regulations like GDPR, HIPAA, and industry-specific standards mandate that organizations maintain detailed records of who accessed sensitive data, how it was accessed, and from which device. Comprehensive identity management platforms integrate logging and auditing capabilities, making it easier for organizations to demonstrate compliance. These systems can produce reports showing device enrollment histories, authentication events, and policy enforcement actions, providing the transparency needed for regulatory audits and security assessments.

As mobile and IoT devices become more integrated into everyday business operations, the need for effective identity management solutions will only grow. By implementing strong enrollment processes, leveraging advanced authentication techniques, and maintaining continuous visibility into device activity, organizations can ensure that their mobile and IoT endpoints remain secure. This approach not only reduces risk but also enables businesses to fully realize the benefits of mobile and IoT technologies—greater flexibility, improved efficiency, and enhanced innovation—without compromising on security or compliance.

Self-Service Capabilities in Cloud Identity

Self-service capabilities have become a cornerstone of modern cloud identity solutions, empowering users to handle many routine tasks independently without relying on IT support. By providing intuitive, user-friendly interfaces for tasks such as password resets, access requests, and profile updates, self-service capabilities enhance productivity, reduce help desk costs, and improve the overall user experience. As organizations move their identity infrastructure to the cloud, implementing robust self-service features is critical for streamlining operations, maintaining security, and supporting an agile workforce.

One of the most common self-service functions is password management. Forgotten passwords are a frequent source of help desk calls, causing frustration for users and creating a significant administrative burden for IT teams. Self-service password reset (SSPR) tools allow users to securely reset their own passwords, often through a series of identity verification steps such as answering security questions, receiving a one-time code via email or SMS, or using biometric authentication. By enabling users to regain access without contacting the help desk, SSPR not only reduces downtime but also enhances security by enforcing stronger password policies and encouraging the use of multifactor authentication.

Access requests and approval workflows are another area where self-service capabilities can deliver significant benefits. Traditionally, employees had to submit access requests through manual processes or email chains, often waiting days or weeks for approvals. Self-service access portals streamline this process by allowing users to view a catalog of available applications and resources, request access with a few clicks, and track the status of their requests in real-time. Automated workflows ensure that requests are routed to the appropriate approvers and that access is granted or denied promptly. This approach improves efficiency, reduces delays, and provides transparency for both users and administrators.

Profile management is another important self-service feature. Users can update their contact information, job titles, or departmental details without needing IT intervention. Having accurate, up-to-date identity information is critical for maintaining security policies, ensuring proper group memberships, and applying role-based access controls. Self-service profile management empowers users to take ownership of their data while ensuring that identity records remain current, which simplifies administrative tasks and reduces the likelihood of errors.

Cloud identity platforms also extend self-service capabilities to mobile devices, enabling users to manage their identities on the go. Mobile apps or responsive web portals allow employees to reset passwords, approve access requests, and update profiles directly from their smartphones or tablets. This level of convenience is particularly valuable for distributed or remote workforces, where users may not have immediate access to a traditional desktop environment. By providing self-service functionality on mobile devices, organizations enhance flexibility, improve user satisfaction, and maintain productivity even when employees are away from their primary workstations.

For IT and security teams, self-service capabilities provide the added benefit of centralized oversight and control. Although users can perform many tasks independently, administrators retain the ability to set policies, define workflows, and monitor activity. For example, IT teams can configure password complexity requirements, enforce multi-factor authentication during certain self-service operations, and ensure that access requests follow established approval hierarchies. Logging and reporting tools also allow administrators to track self-service activities, identify patterns, and address any potential security concerns. This balance of user empowerment and administrative oversight creates a more efficient and secure identity environment.

Self-service capabilities also support regulatory compliance by enabling automated audit trails and ensuring consistent enforcement of policies. For instance, when users request access to a regulated application, the system automatically records who requested access, who approved it, and when the access was granted. This level of documentation is invaluable during compliance audits, providing clear evidence that the organization is adhering to industry standards and legal requirements. Additionally, automated policy enforcement ensures that compliance controls remain active and consistent across all self-service activities, reducing the risk of noncompliance and associated penalties.

As self-service becomes an integral part of cloud identity strategies, organizations can also enhance their onboarding and offboarding processes. When new employees join the company, self-service portals can guide them through initial account setup, including choosing a password, enrolling in multi-factor authentication, and requesting access to the applications they need. For offboarding, self-service tools can streamline the removal of access rights, ensuring that departing employees no longer have access to company resources. These automated, user-driven processes not only save time but also strengthen security by reducing human error and ensuring that access rights are updated promptly.

In addition to operational benefits, self-service capabilities contribute to a positive user experience and overall satisfaction. Employees appreciate having the autonomy to manage their accounts, resolve issues quickly, and request access without navigating complex workflows or waiting for IT support. This sense of empowerment fosters trust in the organization's identity management systems and encourages users to adopt best practices, such as enabling multi-factor authentication and keeping their profiles up to date. A seamless self-service experience also helps attract and retain talent, as modern employees increasingly expect user-friendly tools that allow them to work efficiently and securely.

Self-service capabilities in cloud identity solutions represent a shift toward more agile, user-centric identity management. By enabling users to handle routine tasks independently, organizations can reduce administrative overhead, improve efficiency, and strengthen security. As the workforce becomes more distributed and digital transformation accelerates, the role of self-service in cloud identity will continue to grow, driving productivity, compliance, and user satisfaction.

Identity Orchestration and Policy Enforcement

Identity orchestration and policy enforcement are crucial components of a modern identity and access management strategy. As organizations increasingly rely on multiple identity providers, cloud platforms, and third-party services, the complexity of managing identities and enforcing policies has grown significantly. Identity orchestration provides a framework for seamlessly integrating diverse identity sources, automating workflows, and ensuring that policies are consistently applied across all environments. By streamlining identity processes and embedding security controls at every stage, organizations can improve operational efficiency, enhance security, and maintain compliance with regulatory requirements.

At its core, identity orchestration involves connecting and coordinating multiple identity systems to deliver a unified experience. Many enterprises use a combination of on-premises directories, cloud-based identity providers, and SaaS applications. Without orchestration, each of these systems operates in a silo, making it difficult to manage identities consistently. Identity orchestration platforms bridge these silos by providing a single point of control that integrates with all identity sources, enabling centralized management of user authentication, authorization, and provisioning. This unified approach ensures that users have a seamless experience regardless of which identity provider or application they use.

A key benefit of identity orchestration is its ability to automate complex workflows. Traditionally, identity-related tasks such as provisioning new accounts, revoking access, or updating permissions required manual intervention. With orchestration, these processes are streamlined through predefined workflows that run automatically when certain conditions are met. For example, when a new employee joins a company, the orchestration engine can automatically provision accounts in all necessary systems, assign the correct roles, and ensure that the user is enrolled in multi-factor authentication. Similarly, when an employee changes roles or leaves the organization, their access rights can be adjusted or revoked without any manual input. This automation reduces administrative overhead, increases consistency, and speeds up the overall process.

Policy enforcement is another critical aspect of identity orchestration. As organizations scale, maintaining consistent security policies across multiple environments becomes increasingly challenging. Each application or platform may have its own set of controls and configurations, leading to inconsistencies and potential security gaps. Identity orchestration platforms provide a centralized policy engine that applies uniform security rules to all connected systems. This ensures that policies such as multi-factor authentication, conditional access, and least-privilege access are enforced consistently, regardless of where the user is logging in or what application they are accessing.

Conditional access policies are particularly important in today's hybrid and multi-cloud environments. With identity orchestration, organizations can define policies that take into account contextual factors such as the user's location, device type, time of access, and risk level. For instance, a policy might require additional verification steps for users logging in from unfamiliar locations or devices that do not meet security standards. By continuously evaluating these conditions and adjusting access requirements accordingly, identity orchestration ensures that security is always aligned with the current risk environment.

Another advantage of identity orchestration is improved visibility and reporting. By centralizing identity management and policy enforcement, organizations gain a comprehensive view of all identity-related activities. This visibility enables security teams to monitor authentication patterns, detect anomalies, and identify potential threats. Orchestration platforms typically include dashboards and analytics tools that provide insights into how identities are being used, which policies are being enforced, and where potential vulnerabilities may exist. This data-driven approach helps organizations make informed decisions about their identity strategy, strengthen security posture, and quickly respond to emerging threats.

Identity orchestration also supports compliance efforts by ensuring that policies are consistently applied and that every action is recorded. Many industries are subject to stringent regulatory requirements that mandate detailed logs of who accessed what, when, and how. Orchestration platforms generate these logs automatically, creating a reliable audit trail that demonstrates compliance with frameworks such as GDPR, HIPAA, and PCI DSS. By automating policy enforcement and maintaining comprehensive records, organizations can simplify audits, reduce the risk of noncompliance, and maintain trust with customers and regulators.

Integrating advanced security measures into the orchestration process further enhances its value. Modern identity orchestration platforms can incorporate adaptive authentication, risk-based policies, and behavioral analytics. Adaptive authentication adjusts the level of verification required based on the current risk, ensuring that low-risk users enjoy a smooth experience while high-risk scenarios trigger additional checks. Behavioral analytics help identify unusual patterns that might indicate a compromised account or insider threat. By combining these advanced capabilities with automated policy enforcement, identity orchestration delivers both convenience and security.

As identity environments grow more complex, scalability is another critical consideration. Identity orchestration platforms are designed to handle large-scale operations, accommodating thousands or even millions of identities across multiple systems. By automating workflows and centralizing policy enforcement, these platforms ensure that identity processes remain efficient and secure even as the organization expands. This scalability not only reduces administrative burden but also enables organizations to adopt new technologies, integrate additional applications, and onboard new users without significant disruption.

In addition to operational benefits, identity orchestration and policy enforcement improve the user experience. When users encounter consistent security policies and seamless authentication across all systems, their productivity increases. Self-service capabilities, single sign-on, and reduced friction in the login process all contribute to a more positive experience. At the same time, the organization benefits from stronger security, greater compliance, and more efficient identity management processes. By adopting identity orchestration and centralized policy enforcement, businesses can address the challenges of modern identity environments and position themselves for success in an increasingly complex digital landscape.

Data Privacy and Identity Management

Data privacy and identity management have become inseparable in today's interconnected digital world. As organizations process vast amounts of personal data—ranging from customer information to employee records—the need to protect that data while ensuring seamless access has never been greater. Identity management systems serve as the gateway to sensitive data, making them critical for enforcing privacy policies, controlling access, and maintaining compliance with an ever-growing list of regulations. By integrating robust data privacy measures with identity management solutions, organizations can safeguard personal information, build trust, and reduce the risk of data breaches.

One of the foundational principles of data privacy is minimizing the collection and retention of personal information. Identity management plays a central role in enforcing this principle. By tying data access to clearly defined user identities and roles, organizations can limit the collection of unnecessary data and ensure that only authorized personnel can access sensitive information. For example, role-based access control (RBAC) and attribute-based access control (ABAC) allow administrators to assign permissions based on a user's specific job function or contextual attributes, ensuring that no one has broader access than required. This level of granularity not only enhances security but also helps comply with privacy regulations that mandate data minimization.

Access transparency is another critical aspect of data privacy. Users are increasingly concerned about how their personal information is used, stored, and shared. Modern identity management platforms provide the tools needed to maintain detailed logs of who accessed what data, when, and why. By maintaining these logs, organizations can demonstrate accountability, address user inquiries, and resolve disputes related to data usage. Furthermore, these records serve as a valuable resource during regulatory audits, helping organizations prove compliance with data protection laws such as the General Data Protection Regulation (GDPR) and the California Consumer Privacy Act (CCPA).

Consent management is an area where identity and data privacy intersect. Privacy regulations often require organizations to obtain explicit consent from individuals before collecting or processing their data. Identity management solutions can help manage and enforce consent preferences by tying them directly to user accounts. This ensures that users' choices are respected, and that access to their data is governed by clear, documented consent policies. If a user withdraws consent, the identity system can immediately revoke access to the associated data, ensuring that the organization remains compliant and respects the individual's privacy rights.

Data encryption and anonymization are essential tools for protecting privacy, and identity management systems play a critical role in implementing these measures. By integrating with encryption platforms and data masking technologies, identity solutions can enforce policies that ensure sensitive data is encrypted both in transit and at rest. In addition, they can manage access to decryption keys, ensuring that only authorized users can view or interact with sensitive information. This layered approach helps reduce the risk of data exposure, even if an attacker gains access to a database or storage system.

User authentication methods also have a direct impact on data privacy. Strong authentication mechanisms—such as multi-factor authentication (MFA), biometric verification, and adaptive risk-based authentication—reduce the likelihood of unauthorized access. When combined with identity federation and single sign-on (SSO), these methods simplify user access while maintaining strict security controls. By ensuring that only verified identities can access sensitive data, organizations significantly lower the risk of privacy violations. This is especially important in scenarios where multiple parties, such as contractors or third-party vendors, need access to data. Strong identity management practices ensure that every user accessing personal data is properly authenticated and authorized.

Data privacy regulations require organizations to implement processes for handling data subject rights requests, such as access, correction, or deletion of personal information. Identity management systems help facilitate these requests by linking data access directly to user identities. For instance, when a user requests a copy of their personal data or asks for certain information to be deleted, the identity system can quickly locate the relevant records and ensure that the appropriate actions are taken. This streamlined approach not only simplifies compliance but also improves transparency and trust with users.

Identity management also supports privacy by design, a concept that involves embedding privacy considerations into every aspect of data processing and system architecture. By integrating identity solutions early in the design process, organizations can ensure that access controls, data minimization policies, and consent mechanisms are built into their workflows from the start. This proactive approach helps prevent privacy issues before they arise, making it easier to maintain compliance and build trust with customers and stakeholders.

Another key aspect of data privacy is the ability to detect and respond to potential breaches quickly. Identity management systems with advanced monitoring and analytics capabilities can identify unusual access patterns, such as multiple failed login attempts, unauthorized privilege escalations, or access requests from unexpected locations. By detecting these anomalies in real time, organizations can take immediate action to prevent further exposure, notify affected individuals, and report the incident to regulatory authorities as required. This rapid response capability not only mitigates the impact of breaches but also helps maintain compliance with breach notification requirements.

Data privacy and identity management are deeply intertwined, each reinforcing the other's goals. A strong identity management framework provides the controls, transparency, and automation needed to protect sensitive data, maintain user trust, and ensure regulatory compliance. By integrating privacy considerations into identity systems, organizations can create a more secure, transparent, and efficient approach to handling personal information in an increasingly complex digital landscape.

Identity Breaches: Detection and Response

Identity breaches have become one of the most significant threats to organizations in the digital age. Cybercriminals frequently target user credentials, privileged accounts, and identity repositories to gain unauthorized access to critical systems and sensitive data. Once compromised, these identities can be exploited to escalate privileges, move laterally through networks, and carry out advanced attacks. Rapid detection and an effective response are essential to minimize damage, protect data, and maintain trust.

Detecting identity breaches requires continuous monitoring of identity-related activities and the ability to identify anomalies. Modern identity and access management (IAM) solutions often include advanced monitoring and logging capabilities that provide a comprehensive view of authentication attempts, role assignments, and access requests. By analyzing these logs in real-time, organizations can detect unusual patterns—such as a single user attempting multiple failed logins from different IP addresses or a privileged account accessing sensitive resources at odd hours. These anomalies often serve as early warning signs of a breach in progress, prompting security teams to investigate further.

Machine learning and behavioral analytics are valuable tools for detecting identity breaches. These technologies build baseline profiles of normal user behavior, taking into account factors such as login times, frequently accessed resources, and typical geographic locations. When a user's activity deviates significantly from these patterns, the system can flag it as suspicious. For example, if an employee who usually logs in from a single location suddenly accesses systems from multiple countries within a short time frame, it may indicate that their credentials have been stolen. By leveraging machine learning, IAM solutions can quickly identify subtle anomalies that might otherwise go unnoticed, giving organizations a critical edge in identifying breaches before they cause widespread harm.

Privilege misuse is another common indicator of an identity breach. Once attackers gain access to a user account, they often attempt to escalate privileges or access resources beyond the user's normal scope. Effective detection strategies include monitoring changes to role assignments, unexpected privilege escalations, and unauthorized attempts to access restricted systems. Identity governance tools can automatically flag these changes and send alerts to administrators, enabling swift action to contain potential breaches.

The response to an identity breach must be swift and coordinated. The first step is containment—immediately isolating the compromised accounts, revoking their access, and preventing further unauthorized activity. This may involve disabling accounts, resetting passwords, or implementing temporary access blocks. Containment minimizes the attacker's ability to exploit the compromised identity and limits the potential damage to the organization.

Once the breach is contained, the focus shifts to investigation. Security teams must determine how the breach occurred, identify the entry points used by the attackers, and understand the extent of the compromise. This often involves reviewing audit logs, analyzing network traffic, and examining system configurations. By pinpointing the root cause, organizations can close security gaps and prevent similar incidents in the future.

Communication is another vital component of breach response. Internal stakeholders—such as IT, legal, and executive teams—must be informed of the situation and involved in decision-making. If the breach affects external parties, such as customers or partners, clear and transparent communication is critical. Timely notifications, detailed explanations of what happened, and steps taken to mitigate the issue help maintain trust and demonstrate a commitment to security.

Regulatory requirements also play a significant role in identity breach response. Many jurisdictions have mandatory breach notification laws that dictate how and when affected parties must be informed. IAM solutions with robust auditing and reporting capabilities make it easier to gather the necessary information for these disclosures. By providing detailed records of identity activity, organizations can show regulators that they took appropriate measures to detect, respond to, and mitigate the breach.

Post-incident reviews are essential for improving an organization's security posture. After the immediate response is complete, security teams should conduct a thorough analysis of the breach to identify lessons learned. This may involve reviewing how quickly the breach was detected, how effectively the containment and investigation processes were executed, and what gaps in policies or technologies allowed the breach to occur. The findings from this review should inform updates to identity management policies, enhancements to monitoring tools, and changes to user education programs.

Preventative measures also play a crucial role in minimizing the impact of future identity breaches. Organizations can implement stronger authentication mechanisms, such as multi-factor authentication (MFA) and passwordless solutions, to reduce the likelihood of credential theft. Continuous user education and training help ensure that employees recognize phishing attempts, use strong passwords, and follow best practices for secure access. Additionally, regular access reviews and audits help maintain a clean identity environment, ensuring that users have the appropriate level of access and that dormant accounts are removed.

Identity breaches are a persistent threat that requires vigilance, advanced detection capabilities, and a well-coordinated response strategy. By integrating machine learning, behavioral analytics, and robust monitoring tools into their IAM systems, organizations can detect anomalies earlier and respond more effectively. Clear communication, thorough investigations, and continuous improvement help limit the impact of breaches and strengthen overall security. Through a combination of advanced technology, proactive policies, and a commitment to ongoing learning, organizations can better protect their identities and maintain trust in a constantly evolving threat landscape.

Integration with Cloud Security Tools

As organizations increasingly rely on cloud-based environments, the integration of identity management solutions with advanced cloud security tools has become essential for maintaining a robust security posture. In a cloud-first world, identity plays a central role in defining who or what can access resources, which applications are available, and how data is protected. By seamlessly integrating identity platforms with a broad range of cloud security tools—such as security information and event management (SIEM) systems, cloud access security brokers (CASBs), and workload protection platforms—organizations can ensure consistent policy enforcement, gain greater visibility into user activities, and respond more effectively to potential threats.

One of the primary benefits of integrating identity systems with cloud security tools is enhanced visibility. Traditional on-premises environments typically rely on network-based controls and perimeter defenses to monitor and secure traffic. However, in cloud environments, where resources are highly distributed and users access data from various locations and devices, the network perimeter no longer provides sufficient visibility. Instead, identity becomes the most reliable point of control. By feeding identity-related events—such as login attempts, password changes, privilege escalations, and access denials—into a SIEM solution, organizations can gain a centralized view of all user activity across multiple cloud platforms. This integration enables security teams to quickly detect anomalous behavior, investigate suspicious patterns, and identify emerging threats before they escalate.

Cloud access security brokers (CASBs) also benefit from integration with identity platforms. CASBs act as intermediaries between cloud service users and providers, helping to enforce security policies, monitor data flows, and detect risks. When combined with identity solutions, CASBs can apply granular policies based on user roles, groups, and authentication factors. For instance, a CASB integrated with an identity provider can enforce conditional access policies that allow a user to download sensitive data only if they authenticate using multi-factor authentication or if they are accessing the resource from a trusted device. This level of integration ensures that access controls are not only consistent but also responsive to real-time context, reducing the risk of data exposure or unauthorized access.

Integration with cloud workload protection platforms (CWPPs) is another important aspect of a modern identity-driven security strategy. CWPPs focus on securing workloads—such as virtual machines, containers, and serverless functions—running in cloud environments. By connecting identity management systems to CWPPs, organizations can ensure that only authenticated and authorized users or services can interact with critical workloads. Identity-based controls help prevent unauthorized deployments, modifications, or deletions of workloads, adding an extra layer of protection against insider threats and external attacks. Moreover, integrating identity events into CWPP dashboards provides a more comprehensive understanding of workload security, making it easier to correlate user actions with system changes and detect potential issues early.

Advanced threat detection and response is another area where identity integration with cloud security tools proves invaluable. Modern security operations centers (SOCs) rely on automation, machine learning, and orchestration to analyze vast amounts of data and respond to incidents quickly. Identity systems feed critical context into these tools, helping analysts understand who performed a certain action, what level of access they had, and whether that action aligns with normal user behavior. For example, if a user account suddenly attempts to access a large number of sensitive files outside normal business hours, an integrated security platform can trigger an alert and initiate automated responses—such as temporarily locking the account, requiring additional authentication, or notifying the security team. This streamlined process not only enhances threat detection but also reduces the time it takes to contain and remediate incidents.

Integration also simplifies compliance and reporting. Many industries and regulatory frameworks require organizations to demonstrate that they have implemented adequate access controls, maintained detailed logs of user activity, and responded promptly to security incidents. By consolidating identity data with logs from other security tools, organizations can produce unified reports that provide clear evidence of compliance. This centralized approach makes it easier to pass audits, address compliance inquiries, and show regulators that proper controls are in place.

Furthermore, integration between identity platforms and cloud security tools improves the efficiency of security teams. When identity events are automatically correlated with data from firewalls, endpoint protection solutions, and cloud-native security services, security teams can spend less time piecing together information from disparate sources. Instead, they can focus on higher-value activities—such as threat hunting, policy refinement, and proactive risk management. This improved efficiency not only enhances the organization's overall security posture but also enables faster response times, reducing the likelihood of prolonged incidents.

As cloud environments continue to evolve, so do the tools designed to secure them. Identity integration with these tools ensures that organizations are not only keeping pace with the latest threats but also building a future-proof security framework. By centralizing identity data, applying consistent policies across platforms, and enabling automated responses to suspicious activity, organizations can stay ahead of attackers and maintain trust with their customers, partners, and employees.

Managing Privileged Access in the Cloud

As organizations continue to shift their infrastructure, applications, and data to the cloud, the management of privileged access has become a critical component of overall security strategy. Privileged accounts—those with elevated permissions that allow users to configure systems, deploy applications, and manage data—present an enticing target for attackers. If compromised, these accounts can be used to gain full control of cloud environments, access sensitive information, and disrupt business operations. Ensuring that privileged access is both tightly controlled and continuously monitored is essential for maintaining a secure cloud environment.

One of the most important steps in managing privileged access is identifying all privileged accounts across the cloud environment. These accounts can include administrative users for cloud management consoles, service accounts that run critical processes, and privileged roles within applications or databases. Without a clear inventory, it's impossible to enforce effective access controls or know which accounts pose the greatest risk. Organizations must map out every privileged identity and understand what each account can access and modify. This baseline is the foundation for implementing security policies, monitoring activity, and responding to potential threats.

Once privileged accounts are identified, enforcing the principle of least privilege is key. This means ensuring that each privileged account only has the permissions necessary to perform its specific function and nothing more. In the cloud, it is common for certain accounts or roles to be granted broad, all-encompassing permissions by default. However, these permissions often exceed what is needed, creating unnecessary risk. By carefully reviewing each account's role and adjusting its permissions to the minimum required, organizations can reduce the attack surface. For example, a service account that only needs to read from a storage bucket should not also have write or delete permissions. Applying this principle consistently ensures that even if a privileged account is compromised, the damage it can do is limited.

Multi-factor authentication (MFA) is a fundamental safeguard for privileged access in the cloud. Adding a second layer of authentication—such as a mobile device prompt or a hardware token—makes it significantly harder for attackers to use stolen credentials. Most major cloud providers support MFA for administrative accounts, and enabling this feature is one of the simplest yet most effective ways to protect privileged identities. MFA ensures that even if an attacker obtains a privileged user's password, they cannot easily access the account without the additional authentication factor. For particularly sensitive accounts, requiring multiple layers of MFA or step-up authentication under certain conditions adds further protection.

Privileged access management (PAM) solutions are another critical component of managing privileged accounts in the cloud. These tools provide centralized control over privileged credentials, allowing organizations to enforce strict policies, manage session recordings, and automate credential rotation. With PAM, passwords for privileged accounts are never directly shared with users. Instead, users request access through the PAM platform, which provides temporary credentials for a specific session. This approach reduces the risk of credential leakage, ensures that all privileged access is logged and auditable, and makes it easier to detect unusual activity.

Monitoring and auditing are essential for managing privileged access effectively. Continuous monitoring of privileged accounts allows organizations to detect suspicious behavior early. For instance, if a privileged account suddenly starts accessing resources it has never interacted with before or if it is used at unusual times, these actions can trigger alerts. Real-time visibility into privileged activity, combined with detailed logging, enables security teams to investigate incidents quickly, identify the root cause, and prevent further misuse. Moreover, maintaining an audit trail of privileged access is often a regulatory requirement. Regularly reviewing these logs helps ensure compliance and provides valuable insights for improving security policies over time.

In addition to monitoring human user accounts, organizations must also address privileged access by non-human identities, such as service accounts, API keys, and automated scripts. These accounts often have significant permissions and can be more difficult to secure because they operate without direct user involvement. Implementing strong authentication measures—such as using certificates or managed service identities—reduces the risk of these non-human accounts being misused. Automated rotation of credentials and integration with IAM policies help ensure that these accounts remain secure and that access is tightly controlled.

Another important consideration is implementing just-in-time (JIT) access for privileged roles. With JIT access, elevated permissions are only granted for a limited time and are automatically removed once the task is completed. This approach minimizes the window of opportunity for attackers to exploit privileged accounts and ensures that privileges are not left unnecessarily enabled. JIT access also helps enforce compliance with internal policies and external regulations by providing a clear, time-bound record of when privileged access was granted and why.

Education and training are critical components of any privileged access management strategy. Privileged users must understand the risks associated with their accounts, recognize signs of phishing attempts, and follow best practices for secure authentication. Providing regular training sessions and security updates ensures that administrators, developers, and other privileged users remain aware of the latest threats and know how to respond. Educated users are less likely to fall victim to social engineering attacks and more likely to follow security protocols that protect the organization's cloud environment.

Effective privileged access management in the cloud requires a multi-layered approach that combines strong authentication, least-privilege enforcement, continuous monitoring, and automation. By implementing these strategies, organizations can mitigate the risks associated with privileged accounts, maintain control over critical resources, and protect sensitive data in an increasingly complex cloud landscape.

Identity Proofing and Verification Techniques

In an era where digital interactions dominate personal and professional exchanges, the ability to accurately verify and confirm the identities of individuals and devices has become a cornerstone of modern security frameworks. Identity proofing and verification techniques form the foundation for ensuring that the person or entity claiming an identity is, in fact, legitimate. By establishing trust at the very outset of any digital interaction, organizations can mitigate fraud, protect sensitive information, and maintain compliance with regulatory requirements.

Identity proofing is the process of determining if a claimed identity truly corresponds to a real person. This often involves collecting and verifying personal data, such as name, date of birth, and government-issued identifiers. One of the most common methods is document-based verification, where users are required to provide a copy of an official ID—such as a driver's license or passport—along with supporting documents, such as a utility bill or bank statement. Advanced document verification techniques use optical character recognition (OCR) and machine learning algorithms to validate the authenticity of these documents. By analyzing security features, comparing data against known templates, and cross-referencing with external databases, these solutions can quickly confirm the legitimacy of the presented credentials.

Biometric verification adds another layer of assurance. By leveraging unique physical or behavioral characteristics—such as fingerprints, facial features, voice patterns, or even typing dynamics—biometric methods ensure that the person claiming an identity is physically present and matches the original identity proofed at registration. Modern biometric systems use sophisticated algorithms and sensors to capture and analyze these traits, making them highly resistant to fraud. Facial recognition, for instance, compares a live selfie or video to the photo on a verified ID document, ensuring that the individual presenting the ID is the same person depicted in the document. This real-time confirmation provides a higher level of certainty than traditional methods and is increasingly used in financial services, government portals, and high-security environments.

Knowledge-based verification (KBV) is another widely used technique, although it has limitations. In KBV, individuals must answer a series of questions that only they should know the answers to. These might include details about past addresses, loan amounts, or previous employers. While this approach can be effective, it is increasingly vulnerable to fraud as more personal data becomes accessible through data breaches or social engineering attacks. For this reason, KBV is often combined with other verification methods to strengthen its effectiveness.

The rise of digital identities and federated identity systems has introduced new opportunities for identity proofing and verification. Instead of repeatedly verifying an individual's identity for every service or platform, organizations can rely on a trusted identity provider. These providers perform the initial identity proofing, issuing a digital credential that can be used across multiple services. This approach streamlines the verification process for end-users while ensuring a high standard of security. Technologies such as OpenID Connect and SAML enable these federated identities, allowing seamless integration with various applications and reducing the need for users to manage multiple sets of credentials.

Identity proofing is not a one-time process. As threats evolve and user information changes, ongoing verification is crucial. Continuous identity verification techniques monitor behavior and contextual factors, such as device usage patterns, geographic location, and login times. If an individual's behavior deviates significantly from their established pattern—such as logging in from a new country or using a previously unseen device—additional verification steps can be triggered. These might include re-authenticating through biometrics, answering updated KBV questions, or providing a second form of identification. By integrating continuous verification into the identity lifecycle, organizations maintain a higher level of security without disrupting the user experience.

The use of cryptographic credentials is another advanced technique in identity verification. Public key infrastructure (PKI) and digital certificates allow for strong, cryptographically-backed identity assertions. When users present a certificate signed by a trusted authority, the relying party can verify its authenticity and integrity without direct interaction. This approach is common in secure email communications, digital signatures, and high-assurance environments where identity verification must be both robust and seamless. By leveraging cryptographic techniques, organizations can ensure that credentials are tamper-proof and can be trusted over long periods.

In industries with strict regulatory requirements—such as finance, healthcare, and government—compliance standards often dictate the level of identity proofing and verification necessary. Regulations like the General Data Protection Regulation (GDPR), the Anti-Money Laundering (AML) directives, and the Health Insurance Portability and Accountability Act (HIPAA) require organizations to verify the identities of their users and maintain detailed records of the process. Advanced identity proofing solutions incorporate audit trails, detailed reporting, and ongoing monitoring to meet these compliance obligations. By integrating identity proofing with existing compliance workflows, organizations can streamline the auditing process and reduce the risk of penalties for non-compliance.

Finally, the user experience is a critical consideration in identity proofing and verification. While robust security measures are essential, they must be implemented in a way that does not frustrate or alienate users. Modern identity verification platforms aim to strike a balance between security and convenience. Self-service onboarding, intuitive interfaces, and support for mobile devices help ensure that users can complete the verification process quickly and easily. By reducing friction, these platforms increase user satisfaction, foster trust, and encourage adoption of secure identity practices.

Identity proofing and verification techniques form the bedrock of trust in digital interactions. Through the use of document verification, biometrics, knowledge-based methods, continuous monitoring, cryptographic credentials, and federated identity systems, organizations can ensure that individuals are who they claim to be. By combining these techniques with a user-centric approach and strong compliance measures, businesses can create a secure, seamless, and trustworthy identity environment.

Scaling Identity for Enterprise Growth

As enterprises grow, their identity and access management (IAM) needs become increasingly complex. A growing workforce, expanding partner networks, and a surge in applications and services all place significant demands on identity infrastructure. Scaling identity management to meet these demands requires more than simply increasing capacity; it involves adopting strategies and technologies that maintain security, ensure compliance, and deliver a seamless experience for users. By carefully planning for scalability, organizations can keep their IAM systems agile, secure, and capable of supporting ongoing growth.

One of the main challenges in scaling identity management is the sheer number of identities that must be managed. As organizations hire more employees, onboard contractors, integrate with partners, and deploy new applications, the volume of user accounts, roles, and permissions increases exponentially. To handle this growth, companies must transition from manual or semi-automated processes to fully automated solutions. Automated provisioning and deprovisioning workflows enable identity managers to handle large volumes of accounts quickly and accurately. By integrating these workflows with HR systems, organizations ensure that new hires receive access to the right resources immediately, and that access is promptly removed when an individual leaves the company.

The shift to cloud-based identity solutions is a critical step in scaling IAM systems. Traditional on-premises IAM tools can struggle to keep up with the demands of a rapidly growing enterprise. They often require significant hardware investments and complex configurations that become unwieldy at scale. Cloud identity platforms, on the other hand, provide the flexibility and scalability needed to support enterprise growth. By leveraging the elastic nature of the cloud, organizations can quickly scale their IAM capabilities up or down as needed, without the need for costly infrastructure upgrades. This flexibility allows businesses to maintain consistent security policies and user experiences, even as their workforce and partner ecosystems expand.

Federated identity is another essential component of scaling IAM systems. As enterprises grow, they often acquire new business units, enter joint ventures, or collaborate with external organizations. Each of these entities may have its own identity directory, authentication methods, and access control policies. Federated identity solutions enable seamless integration across these diverse environments. By establishing trust relationships between identity providers, enterprises can allow users from different organizations to access shared resources with a single set of credentials. This approach not only reduces the administrative burden of managing multiple identity systems but also enhances the user experience by simplifying authentication.

Centralized identity governance is critical for maintaining control as identity systems scale. With more users and applications comes greater complexity in managing access rights and permissions. Without proper governance, enterprises risk over-provisioning privileges, creating security gaps, and failing compliance audits. Identity governance platforms provide a unified view of all access rights across the organization, enabling administrators to enforce consistent policies, perform regular access reviews, and ensure that all identities are in compliance with regulatory standards. These governance frameworks help maintain a balance between scalability and security, ensuring that growth does not lead to unchecked access or potential breaches.

Scaling IAM systems also requires robust monitoring and analytics capabilities. As the number of identities and transactions increases, so does the potential for security incidents and compliance violations. Advanced monitoring tools that integrate with IAM platforms provide real-time visibility into user activity, allowing organizations to detect anomalies and respond quickly to potential threats. Machine learning and behavioral analytics further enhance monitoring efforts by identifying patterns and predicting potential risks before they occur. By incorporating these capabilities into their IAM strategy, enterprises can maintain a secure and resilient identity environment as they grow.

Another important aspect of scaling identity management is supporting diverse authentication methods. As organizations expand, they often need to accommodate a broader range of users and devices. This may include employees working remotely, contractors accessing resources from various locations, and partners logging in from different regions. To meet these needs, IAM systems must offer flexible authentication options, such as multi-factor authentication (MFA), passwordless authentication, and biometrics. By providing multiple authentication methods, enterprises can ensure that all users have secure and convenient access, regardless of their location or device.

Scaling identity for enterprise growth also involves addressing non-human identities. As organizations adopt more automated processes, DevOps practices, and Internet of Things (IoT) devices, the number of non-human identities—such as service accounts, APIs, and connected devices—increases. Managing these identities is as critical as managing human users. Enterprises need solutions that can handle large numbers of machine-to-machine interactions, enforce least-privilege access, and rotate credentials automatically. By integrating non-human identity management into their IAM strategy, companies can maintain control over their growing digital ecosystem.

Finally, user experience must remain a priority as identity systems scale. With more users, applications, and authentication requirements, it's easy for IAM processes to become cumbersome. However, a poor user experience can lead to decreased productivity, security workarounds, and increased support requests. IAM platforms that focus on user-centric design—offering single sign-on (SSO), self-service password resets, and intuitive user interfaces—can help maintain user satisfaction even as the system grows in complexity. Ensuring that the IAM solution remains easy to use, even at scale, supports both productivity and security goals.

Scaling identity for enterprise growth requires a strategic approach that encompasses automation, cloud adoption, federation, governance, monitoring, diverse authentication, and user experience. By addressing these areas proactively, organizations can ensure that their IAM systems remain agile, secure, and capable of supporting continued expansion. With the right tools and strategies in place, enterprises can navigate the challenges of scaling identity management while maintaining robust security and delivering a seamless experience for users.

Identity Management in Regulated Industries

In regulated industries such as healthcare, finance, and government, identity management plays a critical role in ensuring compliance, protecting sensitive data, and maintaining public trust. Regulatory frameworks often impose strict requirements on how identities are verified, how access is controlled, and how user activity is monitored. Failure to comply with these regulations can result in severe penalties, reputational damage, and legal consequences. As a result, organizations operating in regulated sectors must adopt robust identity and access management (IAM) solutions that not only meet compliance standards but also enhance security and operational efficiency.

One of the key challenges in regulated industries is ensuring that only authorized individuals have access to sensitive information and critical systems. Identity management serves as the foundation for enforcing access control policies that align with regulatory requirements. By implementing role-based access control (RBAC) and attribute-based access control (ABAC), organizations can ensure that users only have access to the resources they need to perform their duties. For example, a financial institution may limit traders' access to trading platforms, while granting broader permissions to compliance officers. Similarly, a healthcare provider might restrict access to patient records to only those doctors and nurses who are directly involved in a patient's care. These granular access controls help prevent unauthorized access, reduce the risk of insider threats, and maintain compliance with industry regulations.

Another critical aspect of identity management in regulated industries is ensuring the integrity and confidentiality of personal data. Regulations such as the General Data Protection Regulation (GDPR) and the Health Insurance Portability and Accountability Act (HIPAA) require organizations to implement strict data protection measures. Identity management solutions play a key role by enforcing strong authentication methods, encrypting sensitive information, and maintaining detailed audit trails of all identity-related activities. Multi-factor authentication (MFA) is often mandated by regulators, ensuring that even if credentials are compromised, unauthorized access is still prevented. In addition, identity providers that support encryption at rest and in transit help ensure that personal data remains secure throughout its lifecycle.

Auditing and reporting are critical components of compliance in regulated industries. Most regulatory frameworks require organizations to demonstrate that they are following established security policies, regularly reviewing access rights, and documenting any changes to user accounts or roles. Identity management solutions provide the logging and reporting capabilities needed to meet these requirements. By maintaining comprehensive records of user activity—such as login attempts, privilege changes, and access requests—organizations can generate the reports needed for regulatory audits. These logs not only show compliance but also help identify potential security gaps and allow organizations to address them proactively.

Identity lifecycle management is another important consideration. In regulated industries, the process of onboarding new employees, updating their access rights as they change roles, and promptly revoking access when they leave the organization must be well-defined and strictly followed. IAM solutions automate these processes, reducing the likelihood of human error and ensuring that access rights remain accurate and up-to-date. For instance, if a compliance officer moves to a different department, their old privileges can be automatically removed and new permissions applied, ensuring that their access is always appropriate for their current role. This level of control helps maintain compliance and strengthens the organization's security posture.

Regulations also place a heavy emphasis on verifying the identities of external parties, such as contractors, partners, and vendors. These third parties often require access to sensitive systems or data, and managing their identities effectively is crucial for maintaining compliance. Identity federation and single sign-on (SSO) solutions enable organizations to integrate third-party identities with their own systems, ensuring that all access requests are authenticated and authorized according to policy. By establishing trust relationships with external identity providers, organizations can streamline access for partners while maintaining strict controls over what they can see and do. This approach reduces complexity, improves user experience, and ensures that third-party access complies with regulatory requirements.

Another area of focus in regulated industries is maintaining continuous compliance in the face of evolving threats and changing regulations. Identity management solutions must be flexible and scalable to adapt to new standards, additional security controls, and emerging technologies. Advanced IAM platforms offer features such as adaptive authentication, real-time risk analysis, and integration with security information and event management (SIEM) tools. These capabilities help organizations respond quickly to new threats, ensure that their policies remain effective, and keep pace with regulatory changes. By continuously refining their IAM strategies, organizations can stay ahead of compliance challenges and maintain robust security practices.

Identity governance is especially critical in regulated environments. Regular access reviews, certification campaigns, and policy enforcement ensure that all accounts and roles are properly managed. IAM platforms with built-in governance tools enable administrators to set up automated workflows that review user access on a recurring basis. These workflows provide visibility into who has access to sensitive systems, who approved their access, and whether those permissions still align with regulatory guidelines. If discrepancies are found, administrators can take immediate action to correct them, reducing the risk of non-compliance and enhancing overall security.

Identity management also supports regulatory compliance by integrating with other security and compliance solutions. For example, IAM platforms can feed data into SIEM systems, which provide centralized monitoring and incident response capabilities. By correlating identity events with other security data, organizations gain a more comprehensive view of their compliance posture. Additionally, IAM solutions that integrate with endpoint detection and response (EDR) or data loss prevention (DLP) tools provide additional layers of protection, ensuring that sensitive information remains secure even as it is accessed by authorized users.

Identity management in regulated industries is about more than meeting minimum requirements; it is about building a secure, transparent, and efficient framework that supports both compliance and business goals. By leveraging advanced IAM solutions, organizations can enforce strict access controls, maintain detailed audit trails, and adapt to changing regulations. These practices not only ensure compliance but also reduce risk, improve operational efficiency, and build trust with customers, partners, and regulators alike.

Leveraging AI and ML in Identity Governance

Artificial intelligence (AI) and machine learning (ML) have begun transforming the field of identity governance, offering innovative approaches to managing and securing user identities in complex, dynamic environments. As organizations deal with increasing numbers of users, applications, and data sources, traditional static rules and manual processes struggle to keep pace. AI and ML provide the means to automate decision-making, detect anomalies, and adapt identity governance policies in real time, improving both security and operational efficiency. By incorporating these technologies into their identity strategies, organizations can achieve greater agility, more accurate risk assessments, and more effective compliance.

One of the most significant contributions of AI and ML in identity governance is the ability to automate access decisions. Traditionally, identity governance relies on predefined roles, attribute-based policies, and static certifications to determine who can access what. However, these methods require ongoing human intervention to update roles, review access rights, and maintain policy accuracy. With AI-driven solutions, organizations can shift to a more dynamic approach. Machine learning algorithms analyze user behavior, historical access patterns, and contextual factors to predict which permissions are appropriate for each individual. For example, AI can recommend granting access to a new application based on a user's past interactions, department, and peers' access levels, reducing the time and effort involved in provisioning.

AI and ML also enhance the accuracy of access reviews and certification campaigns. In traditional identity governance, periodic access reviews often result in rubber-stamping or overlooking outdated permissions. This can lead to over-provisioning and increased security risks. By leveraging machine learning models, organizations can automatically identify high-risk accounts, unused permissions, and roles that no longer align with current job responsibilities. These models detect patterns that human reviewers might miss, enabling more targeted and meaningful certifications. Security teams can then focus their efforts on the most critical issues, improving the overall effectiveness of the review process.

Anomaly detection is another key benefit of using AI and ML in identity governance. Human behavior and business processes are not static; they change over time due to new projects, organizational restructuring, or shifts in user roles. Static rules often fail to detect unusual behavior until it's too late. Machine learning models, on the other hand, continuously analyze data and adapt to evolving patterns. By establishing a baseline of normal user activity, these models can flag anomalies such as unusual login locations, atypical access times, or unexpected resource usage. When anomalies are detected, the system can trigger alerts, prompt additional authentication steps, or initiate a review of the affected accounts. This proactive approach helps organizations identify potential threats before they cause significant damage.

AI and ML also enable a more nuanced approach to risk scoring. In traditional identity governance, risk assessments often rely on static factors like the sensitivity of an application or the number of privileged accounts. While these factors remain important, they provide only a partial view of the overall risk landscape. Machine learning models incorporate a wider range of data, including user behavior, historical incidents, and contextual information such as location or device type. By continuously learning from new data, these models refine their risk calculations over time. The result is more accurate and dynamic risk scores that better reflect the current threat environment.

Organizations can use these scores to prioritize remediation efforts, enforce stricter controls on high-risk users, and allocate resources more effectively.

In addition to improving security, AI and ML can streamline compliance efforts. Many industries require organizations to maintain detailed records of who has access to what and to demonstrate that access reviews are performed regularly. Machine learning algorithms can simplify this process by automatically identifying which accounts and permissions are most likely to be flagged during an audit. By focusing on these high-risk areas, organizations can ensure that their compliance efforts are both thorough and efficient. Moreover, AI-driven reporting tools can generate clear, actionable insights, making it easier for compliance teams to prepare for audits and provide evidence of continuous oversight.

AI and ML also support the principle of least privilege, which is fundamental to effective identity governance. Ensuring that users have only the access they need—and nothing more—is a challenging task, particularly in large, complex environments. Machine learning models can analyze which permissions are actually used and recommend the removal of excess privileges. By dynamically adjusting access levels based on real-world usage patterns, organizations can enforce least privilege more consistently. This reduces the attack surface, limits the potential impact of compromised accounts, and strengthens overall security.

As the adoption of AI and ML in identity governance grows, these technologies are becoming more accessible and easier to integrate into existing frameworks. Many modern identity governance platforms now include built-in AI and ML capabilities, enabling organizations to quickly start reaping the benefits. Additionally, AI and ML tools can integrate with other security solutions, such as security information and event management (SIEM) systems and endpoint protection platforms, providing a more holistic view of identity-related risks. This integration allows organizations to correlate identity data with broader security events, improving incident detection and response times.

AI and ML are revolutionizing identity governance by automating complex processes, enhancing risk management, and enabling a more proactive approach to securing user identities. These technologies empower organizations to adapt to rapidly changing environments, address emerging threats, and maintain compliance with evolving regulations. By embracing AI and ML, businesses can build a more resilient, efficient, and secure identity governance framework that keeps pace with today's demands.

Identity Continuity During Migrations

Migrating to new systems, platforms, or cloud environments often presents one of the most significant challenges organizations face in maintaining uninterrupted identity management. As businesses adopt new technologies, replace legacy systems, or transition to multi-cloud strategies, ensuring a seamless and secure migration of user identities, roles, and permissions is critical. The process must balance operational continuity with stringent security measures, all while minimizing disruptions for end users. By employing robust strategies and leveraging modern identity management solutions, organizations can ensure a smooth migration that maintains both the integrity and accessibility of their identity infrastructure.

The foundation of identity continuity lies in thorough planning. Before any migration begins, it is essential to understand the current identity landscape fully. This involves creating a detailed inventory of all user accounts, roles, groups, and access permissions in the existing system. Mapping out the dependencies between applications, directories, and identity stores helps identify potential risks and gaps that might arise during the migration. With this knowledge in hand, organizations can develop a clear migration plan that outlines the steps needed to transfer identities, update policies, and verify that all roles and permissions are correctly applied in the new environment.

A critical aspect of identity continuity is preserving authentication mechanisms throughout the migration process. If users are suddenly unable to log in or must reset their credentials after a migration, it can cause significant downtime and frustration. To prevent this, organizations should use identity federation and single sign-on (SSO) solutions that allow users to authenticate seamlessly across old and new environments. Federated identity solutions establish trust relationships between the existing and new identity providers, enabling users to continue using their current credentials without disruption. By integrating both environments under a unified authentication framework, organizations ensure that the migration appears transparent to end users.

In addition to authentication, maintaining consistent access control policies is crucial. During a migration, the underlying infrastructure may change, but the need for secure, role-based access to sensitive data and applications remains constant. Organizations must ensure that all existing access control policies are accurately translated to the new environment. Role-based access control (RBAC) and attribute-based access control (ABAC) policies should be reviewed and updated as needed, ensuring that permissions remain aligned with job functions and business needs. Automated tools that map old roles to new ones, or that validate permissions against existing policies, can greatly simplify this process and reduce errors.

Data integrity and synchronization also play a central role in identity continuity. In many migrations, both the old and new systems must operate in parallel for a period of time. During this coexistence phase, it is critical that user data, group memberships, and role assignments remain synchronized across both environments. Tools and processes that ensure real-time or near-real-time replication of identity data help prevent conflicts, reduce the risk of outdated information, and ensure that users have consistent access regardless of which environment they use. This synchronization also helps maintain compliance with regulatory requirements, as audit trails and access logs remain consistent and traceable throughout the migration.

To ensure continuity, organizations should implement robust testing and validation processes before fully switching over to the new system. Testing involves verifying that all user accounts can successfully authenticate, that access policies are enforced as expected, and that data integrity is maintained across environments. Creating a test environment that mirrors the production setup allows administrators to identify and address issues before they impact end users. Validation steps should include checking that federated authentication is functioning properly, that roles and permissions have been accurately mapped, and that audit logs are correctly recording activity. By thoroughly testing and validating the new environment, organizations can minimize disruptions and ensure a smooth transition.

Another consideration for identity continuity during migrations is maintaining transparency with end users. Communication plays a vital role in building trust and reducing confusion. Users should be informed about what to expect during the migration process, including any changes to how they access applications or services. Providing clear instructions, support resources, and a reliable channel for reporting issues helps ensure that users remain productive and confident in the transition. Transparency also reduces the likelihood of users resorting to insecure workarounds, such as sharing credentials or using unauthorized tools.

Security must remain a top priority throughout the migration. Identity migrations can be an attractive target for attackers, as the process often involves changes to authentication mechanisms, increased administrative activity, and temporary coexistence of multiple systems. To mitigate these risks, organizations should implement multi-factor authentication (MFA) for all privileged accounts and consider extending MFA requirements to all users during the migration. Enhanced monitoring and logging should be in place to detect any unusual activity, such as unexpected login attempts, unauthorized role changes, or excessive permissions being granted. By maintaining strong security measures, organizations can safeguard user identities and reduce the risk of breaches during the migration.

Finally, post-migration reviews and optimizations help ensure long-term identity continuity. Once the migration is complete, organizations should conduct a thorough review to confirm that all accounts, roles, and permissions have been successfully transferred and that the new environment is functioning as intended. Any discrepancies or issues identified during this review should be addressed promptly. Additionally, organizations can use this opportunity to optimize their identity governance processes, improve access controls, and implement more efficient policies. By taking a proactive approach to post-migration maintenance, businesses can maintain a secure and stable identity environment that supports their ongoing growth and operational needs.

Security Assessments and Identity Health Checks

Maintaining a robust and secure identity management environment requires ongoing evaluation and continuous improvement. Security assessments and identity health checks are essential tools for organizations aiming to ensure that their identity systems remain resilient, compliant, and aligned with industry best practices. These evaluations help identify weaknesses, uncover potential vulnerabilities, and provide actionable recommendations for strengthening identity security. By conducting regular assessments and health checks, organizations can stay ahead of emerging threats, maintain compliance with regulatory requirements, and safeguard sensitive information.

The primary goal of security assessments is to determine the overall effectiveness of an organization's identity and access management (IAM) framework. A comprehensive assessment involves examining various components of the IAM ecosystem, including user authentication processes, access control policies, identity governance procedures, and directory configurations. This holistic approach allows security teams to identify gaps in their current practices and address issues before they can be exploited by malicious actors. For instance, an assessment might reveal outdated password policies, excessive administrative privileges, or inconsistent role assignments—issues that could increase the risk of credential theft or unauthorized access.

Identity health checks focus on the operational integrity of identity systems. They evaluate the consistency and accuracy of user account data, group memberships, and role assignments. Health checks often involve verifying that user attributes are properly synchronized across all systems, that inactive accounts are promptly deactivated, and that permissions remain aligned with current job responsibilities. By regularly performing identity health checks, organizations can reduce the likelihood of privilege creep—where users accumulate excessive permissions over time—and ensure that their IAM environment remains well-organized and secure.

One key aspect of security assessments is the identification of high-risk accounts and roles. Privileged accounts, such as administrators or service accounts with elevated permissions, are prime targets for attackers. Security assessments help pinpoint these accounts, evaluate how they are being used, and determine whether additional safeguards are needed. For example, an assessment might uncover an administrator account that lacks multi-factor authentication (MFA) or a service account that has not had its credentials rotated in years. By identifying these high-risk accounts, organizations can implement stronger controls, such as requiring MFA, enforcing regular credential rotations, or applying just-in-time access.

Another critical component of both assessments and health checks is reviewing the effectiveness of authentication mechanisms. Strong authentication is the first line of defense against identity-related attacks. Security assessments often include an analysis of current authentication methods—such as passwords, MFA, and biometric solutions—and evaluate whether they meet modern security standards. If an organization is still relying solely on passwords, an assessment may recommend introducing MFA or exploring passwordless authentication options. Identity health checks complement this effort by ensuring that authentication configurations are consistently applied across all systems and that any changes are properly documented.

In addition to examining authentication, assessments also focus on access control policies. Effective IAM systems enforce the principle of least privilege, granting users only the permissions they need to perform their job functions. Security assessments review existing access control rules, role definitions, and policy configurations to ensure they align with organizational goals and regulatory requirements. If a policy is overly permissive or outdated, the assessment provides clear guidance on how to refine it. Identity health checks then verify that these policies are consistently enforced and that any deviations are promptly addressed.

Auditing and logging are another area where security assessments and health checks play a crucial role. Comprehensive logging and monitoring are essential for detecting suspicious activity and responding to security incidents. Assessments evaluate whether logging mechanisms are properly configured, whether logs are retained for an appropriate duration, and whether they are accessible for analysis. Identity health checks ensure that logs accurately reflect user activities, that they are correlated with other security data sources, and that alerts are being generated for abnormal behavior. Together, these evaluations help organizations maintain a strong audit trail, improve incident detection, and support compliance requirements.

Compliance and regulatory considerations are a central focus of security assessments. Many industries have strict guidelines for identity management, such as requiring regular access reviews, documenting changes to user accounts, and enforcing robust authentication methods. Security assessments identify any gaps between the organization's current IAM practices and regulatory requirements. They provide actionable recommendations for closing those gaps, reducing the risk of compliance violations and associated penalties. Identity health checks complement this process by ensuring that compliance-related configurations—such as mandatory password policies, data retention periods, and role-based access rules—are consistently applied and regularly reviewed.

The benefits of regular security assessments and identity health checks extend beyond compliance and risk mitigation. These evaluations also support continuous improvement and long-term IAM strategy. By gaining insight into current weaknesses, organizations can prioritize investments in new technologies, streamline processes, and enhance user experience. For instance, an assessment might reveal that certain identity workflows are overly complex, leading to user frustration and increased help desk calls. The resulting recommendations can help streamline those workflows, improving both efficiency and satisfaction.

Security assessments and identity health checks are not one-time activities; they are ongoing processes that evolve with the organization's needs and the changing threat landscape. Conducting these evaluations on a regular basis ensures that IAM systems remain resilient, that emerging risks are promptly addressed, and that compliance requirements are continuously met. By embedding these practices into their overall security program, organizations can maintain strong identity controls, improve operational efficiency, and confidently navigate the complexities of modern identity management.

Future Trends in Identity Management Technologies

Identity management technologies are evolving rapidly, driven by the growing complexity of IT environments, the shift to cloud-based services, and an increasing emphasis on user experience and security. As organizations strive to keep pace with changing threats, regulatory requirements, and digital transformation initiatives, they are adopting innovative approaches and tools that go beyond traditional identity and access management (IAM) methods. Several key trends are emerging that promise to shape the future of identity management, enabling organizations to meet these challenges while maintaining a secure, seamless, and scalable identity ecosystem.

One significant trend is the move toward decentralized identity models. Traditional identity management relies heavily on centralized directories and identity providers, which can become bottlenecks and single points of failure. Decentralized identity approaches, built on blockchain and distributed ledger technologies, aim to give users more control over their personal information. With decentralized identity, individuals manage their own credentials—stored in digital wallets— and share only the necessary information with service providers. This approach reduces dependency on central repositories, increases privacy, and offers greater portability across multiple platforms. As the technology matures, decentralized identity is likely to play a larger role in enterprise and consumer identity management.

Passwordless authentication is another trend gaining momentum. Passwords have long been a weak point in security, often reused, stolen, or easily guessed. Organizations are increasingly adopting passwordless methods, such as biometrics, hardware security keys, and cryptographic authentication, to enhance both security and user experience. These approaches rely on stronger factors, such as fingerprint scans or device-based certificates, rather than traditional passwords. As more platforms support passwordless authentication, organizations will find it easier to eliminate password-related vulnerabilities while streamlining the login process for end-users.

The rise of artificial intelligence (AI) and machine learning (ML) is also transforming identity management. These technologies are being used to detect anomalies, predict risks, and automate identity governance. For example, ML models can analyze user behavior patterns to identify unusual activity, such as a user suddenly accessing resources from a new location or attempting to escalate privileges. AI can recommend more efficient access policies, flag outdated roles, and even automate the certification process for access reviews. By incorporating AI and ML into IAM solutions, organizations can enhance their security posture, reduce manual effort, and maintain more accurate and adaptive access controls.

Zero Trust architecture is driving new approaches to identity management. Zero Trust principles emphasize continuous verification and the assumption that no user, device, or network segment should be inherently trusted. In a Zero Trust model, identity is at the center of every access decision. This has led to increased adoption of identity-based segmentation, real-time risk scoring, and adaptive access controls. As organizations implement Zero Trust strategies, they are turning to identity management technologies that can integrate with other security tools, enforce granular policies, and ensure that every access attempt is verified based on current context. The demand for solutions that support Zero Trust principles will continue to grow, pushing identity management platforms to become more dynamic, flexible, and context-aware.

The shift to multi-cloud and hybrid environments is also shaping the future of identity management. Many organizations now operate across multiple cloud providers and maintain a mix of on-premises and cloud-based resources. This diversity creates complexity in managing identities and permissions. Identity federation, single sign-on (SSO), and cross-cloud identity orchestration are becoming critical capabilities. Advanced IAM solutions must handle identities across disparate platforms, ensure consistent enforcement of policies, and provide unified visibility into access activity. As hybrid and multi-cloud environments become the norm, identity management tools that can seamlessly bridge these ecosystems will become increasingly essential.

Another important trend is the integration of identity management with broader security and compliance frameworks. IAM is no longer viewed in isolation but as a key component of an organization's overall cybersecurity strategy. Modern identity solutions are being designed to integrate with security information and event management (SIEM) systems, endpoint detection and response (EDR) tools, and data protection platforms. By correlating identity events with other security data, organizations gain a more comprehensive understanding of their threat landscape and can respond more quickly to potential incidents. Additionally, tighter integration with compliance tools simplifies auditing, reporting, and enforcement of regulatory requirements.

User experience (UX) is becoming a central focus of identity management innovation. As organizations compete to attract and retain talent, they are investing in IAM solutions that provide a frictionless experience for employees, contractors, and customers. Features such as seamless SSO, self-service account management, and intuitive interfaces are no longer optional—they are expected. Emerging technologies, like adaptive authentication and contextual access controls, further enhance the user experience by dynamically adjusting security requirements based on the user's current situation. By prioritizing UX, organizations can improve productivity, reduce help desk calls, and strengthen security by encouraging compliance with best practices.

The integration of non-human identities—such as service accounts, APIs, and IoT devices—into identity management frameworks is another growing trend. As automation, DevOps practices, and connected devices proliferate, organizations must manage a vast array of machine identities. These identities often have significant privileges, making them a prime target for attackers. IAM platforms are evolving to provide better visibility, lifecycle management, and security controls for machine identities. Features like automated credential rotation, role-based permissions for APIs, and real-time monitoring of device behavior are becoming standard. This trend ensures that organizations can maintain strong security even as the number of non-human identities continues to rise.

Finally, privacy-enhancing technologies are gaining importance in the IAM landscape. Regulations such as GDPR, CCPA, and others place strict requirements on how personal data is handled. Identity management solutions are increasingly incorporating privacy-preserving techniques, such as data minimization, encrypted storage, and consent management. Emerging standards and frameworks for decentralized identity and verifiable credentials also support stronger privacy protections. By adopting these technologies, organizations can ensure compliance, build user trust, and demonstrate their commitment to safeguarding personal information.

The future of identity management technologies is marked by innovation and integration. As organizations adapt to new challenges and opportunities, they are embracing decentralized identities, passwordless authentication, AI-driven insights, and Zero Trust architectures. The convergence of IAM with other security and compliance tools, the growing importance of user experience, and the need to manage both human and machine identities are all shaping the next generation of identity solutions. By staying ahead of these trends, organizations can build a secure, scalable, and user-friendly identity ecosystem that supports their long-term goals.

Building an Identity-Centric Security Culture

An organization's security culture is a reflection of how well its people, processes, and technologies align with its security objectives. In today's digital landscape, where identities play a pivotal role in enabling access to critical resources and protecting sensitive data, fostering an identity-centric security culture is essential. Rather than treating identity as a standalone technical component, it must become a foundational element of the organization's overall security mindset. By building a culture that prioritizes identity protection, organizations can not only reduce risk but also empower their workforce, strengthen compliance, and support long-term business growth.

At the heart of an identity-centric security culture is the recognition that every user, device, and application represents a potential point of entry for attackers. This perspective shifts the focus from traditional perimeter-based defenses to identity-based controls. Instead of relying solely on firewalls and network segmentation, organizations place identity at the center of their security strategies, ensuring that every access request is authenticated, authorized, and monitored. This identity-first approach is not just about implementing technology; it is about instilling a mindset throughout the organization that views identity as a primary line of defense.

A strong identity-centric culture begins with clear leadership and a commitment from the top. Senior executives and managers must lead by example, demonstrating that identity security is a strategic priority rather than a checkbox compliance measure. This leadership commitment involves investing in the right identity management tools, setting clear policies, and ensuring that the entire organization understands the importance of protecting identities. When leadership actively promotes identity security, it sends a message that every employee has a role to play in safeguarding sensitive information.

Employee education and training are critical components of building an identity-centric security culture. While technical controls are essential, human behavior often determines the success or failure of those controls. Employees need to understand the role of identity in security, learn how to recognize phishing attempts, and adopt best practices for password hygiene and multi-factor authentication (MFA). Regular training sessions, workshops, and awareness campaigns help embed identity security into daily workflows. Over time, employees become more mindful of their actions and more proactive in safeguarding their accounts, devices, and data.

In addition to educating employees, organizations must create an environment that encourages reporting and collaboration. An open culture where employees feel comfortable reporting suspicious activity or potential vulnerabilities fosters early detection and rapid response. For example, if a team member notices unusual account activity or receives a phishing email, they should know exactly how to report it and trust that their concerns will be taken seriously. This collaborative approach strengthens the organization's overall security posture by ensuring that identity threats are identified and addressed quickly.

Integrating identity management into daily workflows also helps reinforce an identity-centric culture. When employees interact with secure single sign-on (SSO) portals, use self-service password reset tools, or receive automated alerts about unusual login activity, they become more aware of the organization's commitment to protecting identities. By making identity security tools user-friendly and accessible, organizations encourage adoption and increase participation. Over time, these regular interactions help normalize secure behaviors and reinforce the idea that protecting identity is everyone's responsibility.

Establishing metrics and measuring progress is another key aspect of building an identity-centric culture. Organizations should track metrics such as the percentage of employees enrolled in MFA, the frequency of password resets, and the number of reported identity-related incidents. By reviewing these metrics regularly, security teams can identify areas for improvement, highlight successes, and demonstrate the value of an identity-first approach. Transparent reporting also helps maintain momentum, showing employees and leadership alike that their efforts are making a measurable impact.

A crucial component of building this culture is aligning identity security with broader business goals. Security is often seen as a barrier, but when approached through the lens of identity, it becomes an enabler. By streamlining access, improving user experience, and reducing friction, identity-focused initiatives can enhance productivity, support compliance efforts, and strengthen customer trust. Framing identity security as a business enabler helps shift the narrative from "something we have to do" to "something that drives our success." When employees understand that their participation in identity security efforts contributes to the organization's mission, they are more likely to embrace these practices.

Collaboration across departments is also vital. Identity security is not the sole responsibility of the IT or security team; it involves HR, legal, compliance, and even marketing. HR departments play a crucial role in onboarding and offboarding employees, ensuring that identities are provisioned and deprovisioned securely. Legal and compliance teams help define the regulatory requirements and policies that guide identity governance. Marketing and communications teams can help craft effective awareness campaigns and communicate the value of identity-centric initiatives. When these groups work together, the organization creates a cohesive, unified approach to identity security.

An identity-centric security culture is not built overnight; it requires ongoing effort, adaptability, and a long-term commitment to continuous improvement. By embedding identity into every aspect of the organization's operations—through leadership support, employee education, accessible tools, measurable outcomes, and cross-departmental collaboration—companies can create a culture that views identity security not as an afterthought, but as a core pillar of their overall strategy.

Aligning Identity Management with Business Goals

Effective identity management is not just about securing access and enforcing compliance; it is also about enabling business objectives, enhancing user experience, and supporting organizational growth. By aligning identity management strategies with broader business goals, organizations can improve efficiency, reduce risk, and foster innovation. This alignment requires a deep understanding of how identity and access management (IAM) contributes to the organization's mission, as well as ongoing collaboration between technical teams, business stakeholders, and leadership. When identity management initiatives are closely tied to business outcomes, the result is a more agile, secure, and successful enterprise.

A key step in aligning identity management with business goals is defining those goals clearly. Whether the organization's priority is expanding into new markets, improving customer satisfaction, streamlining compliance processes, or accelerating digital transformation, the IAM strategy must reflect these objectives. For example, a company focused on scaling its operations may prioritize scalable, cloud-based identity solutions that can grow alongside the business. By understanding the overarching goals, identity management teams can tailor their initiatives to directly support these outcomes.

User experience plays a crucial role in this alignment. Seamless access to applications and services not only improves productivity but also enhances employee satisfaction and customer trust. When employees can access the tools they need without unnecessary friction, they spend less time dealing with login issues and more time contributing to the company's objectives. Similarly, when customers have a smooth authentication experience—such as through single sign-on (SSO) or passwordless login options—they are more likely to engage with the organization's services. Aligning IAM strategies with the goal of enhancing user experience ensures that identity management efforts actively support the organization's reputation, productivity, and customer loyalty.

Compliance and regulatory requirements often shape business goals, particularly in highly regulated industries. IAM solutions must be designed to meet these requirements while minimizing the burden on end-users and administrators. By aligning identity management initiatives with compliance objectives, organizations can simplify audits, reduce the risk of fines, and maintain trust with customers and partners. For example, an IAM platform that provides automated access reviews and detailed audit trails helps ensure that the company remains compliant without diverting significant resources away from other business priorities. This alignment ensures that security and compliance efforts support, rather than hinder, the organization's overall mission.

Scalability and agility are also critical to aligning identity management with business growth. As organizations expand their workforce, add new applications, or enter new markets, their identity management systems must keep pace. Implementing IAM solutions that can handle increased user loads, support multi-cloud environments, and integrate with diverse platforms enables the organization to grow without encountering identity-related bottlenecks. By planning for scalability from the outset, IAM teams ensure that identity management strategies remain aligned with the organization's growth objectives, allowing the business to remain nimble and responsive in a rapidly changing environment.

Security is another fundamental consideration in aligning identity management with business goals. While security is often seen as a cost center, it can actually be a business enabler when approached strategically. Robust identity security measures—such as multi-factor authentication (MFA), adaptive access controls, and continuous monitoring—reduce the likelihood of data breaches, which can have a devastating impact on business operations, reputation, and financial performance. By integrating these security measures into the IAM framework, organizations create a secure environment that supports innovation, protects intellectual property, and maintains customer trust.

Cross-functional collaboration is essential for ensuring that identity management initiatives align with business goals. IAM teams must work closely with HR, IT, compliance, and business unit leaders to understand their needs and priorities. For instance, HR teams are often involved in the onboarding and offboarding process, making them key stakeholders in identity provisioning and deprovisioning workflows. By collaborating with HR, IAM teams can design processes that not only enhance security but also streamline employee transitions, reducing downtime and improving productivity. Similarly, working with compliance officers ensures that IAM policies address regulatory requirements while remaining practical and enforceable. This cross-functional alignment ensures that identity management efforts directly support the goals of all parts of the organization.

Another important aspect of aligning identity management with business goals is demonstrating return on investment (ROI). IAM teams must be able to show how their initiatives contribute to cost savings, efficiency gains, and risk reduction. For example, implementing an SSO solution may reduce the number of password-related help desk calls, saving time and money for both IT staff and end-users. Likewise, automating access reviews and certifications can free up valuable administrative resources, allowing staff to focus on strategic projects rather than repetitive tasks. By highlighting these benefits, IAM teams can secure the buy-in and support needed to maintain alignment with business objectives.

Continuous improvement is key to maintaining alignment between identity management and business goals. As business priorities evolve, IAM strategies must adapt. Regularly reviewing IAM metrics, gathering feedback from stakeholders, and staying informed about emerging technologies and best practices ensure that identity management remains relevant and effective. This iterative approach allows organizations to refine their IAM initiatives, address new challenges, and maintain a strong connection between identity management and broader business outcomes.

Identity-Driven Incident Response Plans

An effective incident response plan must account for the increasingly central role of identities in modern security breaches. As organizations move towards cloud-first environments, adopt zero trust frameworks, and integrate an array of third-party applications, identity becomes the common thread that links users, devices, and data. Many of today's cyberattacks target credentials, privileged accounts, and identity systems rather than traditional network perimeters. This shift has made it imperative for organizations to incorporate identity management directly into their incident response strategies. Identity-driven incident response plans ensure that security teams can quickly detect, contain, and remediate identity-related breaches while maintaining continuity and trust.

The first step in crafting an identity-driven incident response plan is establishing comprehensive visibility into all identity systems and related activities. This visibility begins with a detailed inventory of identities, including human users, service accounts, application accounts, and non-human entities such as APIs and IoT devices. Security teams must also have access to a centralized view of identity logs, authentication events, privilege escalations, and policy changes. By consolidating this information into a single pane of glass, organizations can quickly identify anomalies, pinpoint the source of incidents, and understand the scope of potential compromise.

Integrating identity monitoring and analytics tools into the incident response process is critical for early detection. Machine learning and behavior analytics can identify unusual patterns that signal an attack, such as an account accessing resources it has never used before, failed login attempts from unexpected locations, or the sudden creation of new privileged accounts. These tools can trigger alerts that inform the incident response team, allowing them to investigate and act before attackers can fully exploit compromised credentials. The use of automation in identity monitoring not only accelerates detection but also reduces the time and effort required to sift through large volumes of identity data.

Once an identity-related incident is detected, a structured containment process is essential. Identity-driven response plans define specific actions to isolate compromised accounts and prevent further damage. For example, if an account shows signs of credential theft, the plan might call for immediately locking the account, forcing a password reset, or requiring additional authentication factors. In cases of privilege escalation, the plan could involve revoking administrative privileges or disabling the account until the incident is resolved. Containment steps must be carefully calibrated to halt the attack without unduly disrupting legitimate business operations.

Communication plays a vital role in the effectiveness of identity-driven incident response plans. During an incident, clear communication channels must be in place so that all relevant teams—security, IT, legal, compliance, and management—are informed and aligned. Security teams need to share real-time updates about what they've detected, what actions they're taking, and what additional support they might need. In regulated industries, compliance officers may need immediate access to logs and evidence to meet reporting requirements. Having predefined communication protocols ensures that everyone knows their role, reduces confusion, and facilitates a coordinated response.

Another critical element of identity-driven incident response is the remediation phase. Once the immediate threat is contained, organizations must work quickly to close the vulnerabilities that allowed the breach to occur. This might involve revoking unused accounts, tightening password policies, implementing multi-factor authentication, or improving role-based access controls. In cases where an identity provider or federated authentication system was exploited, remediation may require reviewing trust relationships, reissuing certificates, or applying software patches. The goal of remediation is not only to restore normal operations but also to strengthen the identity management environment to prevent future incidents.

Post-incident analysis and lessons learned sessions help refine identity-driven response plans over time. After the incident is resolved, the security team should conduct a thorough review to determine what went wrong, what worked well, and what can be improved. This analysis might reveal that certain alerts were too slow, that specific containment steps took longer than expected, or that certain roles and responsibilities were unclear. By incorporating these insights into the plan, organizations can improve response times, enhance coordination, and bolster their overall identity security posture.

Training and preparedness exercises ensure that the incident response plan is actionable and effective when needed. Just as organizations conduct fire drills or simulate network intrusions, they should regularly test their identity-driven response plans. Tabletop exercises, red team/blue team scenarios, and simulated identity breaches help security teams practice their response procedures, identify gaps in the plan, and build confidence in their ability to handle real-world incidents. These exercises also help non-technical stakeholders understand their roles, making the entire organization more prepared and resilient.

An effective identity-driven incident response plan also includes continuous improvement measures. As identity threats evolve and new attack techniques emerge, the plan must be updated to remain relevant. Organizations should review industry best practices, follow guidance from standards bodies such as NIST or ISO, and stay informed about the latest trends in identity-based attacks. By keeping the plan current and aligned with the threat landscape, organizations ensure that their response efforts remain proactive rather than reactive.

Identity-driven incident response plans offer a structured, efficient, and focused approach to handling the growing number of identity-based threats. By emphasizing visibility, early detection, structured containment, clear communication, and continuous improvement, these plans provide a robust framework for protecting critical identities, safeguarding sensitive data, and maintaining trust in today's increasingly complex security environment.

Best Practices for Cloud Identity Resilience

In today's digital-first world, cloud identity resilience is a cornerstone of operational security and business continuity. Organizations depend on the ability of their identity and access management (IAM) systems to withstand failures, recover quickly from disruptions, and maintain secure access at all times. Building a resilient identity infrastructure involves more than simply deploying cloud-based IAM solutions; it requires a comprehensive strategy that considers redundancy, backup processes, recovery mechanisms, and robust governance practices. By implementing the following best practices, organizations can ensure that their cloud identity systems remain reliable, secure, and able to adapt to evolving threats and demands.

One of the foundational best practices for cloud identity resilience is establishing redundant, geographically distributed infrastructure. Relying solely on a single IAM provider or data center creates a significant single point of failure. To address this, organizations should deploy their identity services across multiple regions or availability zones. This geographic dispersion ensures that even if one data center experiences an outage, users can still authenticate and access resources from another location. Redundancy at both the identity provider and directory service levels is critical, as it provides continuity during unexpected disruptions and minimizes downtime.

Regularly backing up identity data and configurations is another essential practice. Cloud IAM solutions often rely on complex configurations, including policies, roles, and group memberships, to enforce access controls. If these configurations are lost or corrupted, the resulting downtime and recovery efforts can be extensive. Organizations should implement automated backup processes that periodically save IAM configurations, user directories, and encryption keys to secure storage. These backups should be stored in multiple locations, both within and outside the primary cloud environment, ensuring that they remain accessible even in the event of a major outage. Testing the restoration process regularly is equally important, as it verifies that backups are complete, accurate, and readily usable in a real-world scenario.

Multi-factor authentication (MFA) and adaptive authentication mechanisms are key to ensuring resilience in the face of credential compromise. With the growing prevalence of phishing and other identity-based attacks, relying solely on passwords for user authentication is no longer sufficient. By requiring additional authentication factors—such as a mobile app push notification, biometric verification, or a hardware security token—organizations significantly reduce the risk of unauthorized access. Adaptive authentication adds another layer of resilience by assessing contextual factors such as user location, device health, and behavioral patterns. If unusual activity is detected, adaptive authentication can trigger additional verification steps, thereby maintaining secure access even when primary credentials are compromised.

Implementing robust monitoring and alerting mechanisms further strengthens identity resilience. Cloud identity solutions generate a wealth of logs and metrics that can provide early warning signs of potential issues. By integrating identity logs with centralized logging and security information and event management (SIEM) systems, organizations gain real-time visibility into authentication events, policy changes, and anomalous user behavior. Security teams can set up automated alerts for suspicious patterns, such as multiple failed login attempts, unusual IP address activity, or unexpected privilege escalations. Proactive monitoring enables quick response to incidents and helps prevent small issues from escalating into major disruptions.

Another best practice is conducting regular access reviews and certifications. Over time, users accumulate permissions as they move between roles, work on different projects, or gain access to new resources. Without regular reviews, this "privilege creep" can lead to excessive permissions and an increased attack surface. Periodic access reviews ensure that users have only the permissions they need, and that unnecessary access rights are revoked. Automated certification campaigns streamline the review process by providing managers and administrators with pre-configured reports, enabling them to quickly validate or adjust access levels. By maintaining a clean and current set of access controls, organizations reduce the risk of identity-related vulnerabilities and improve overall security resilience.

Strong identity governance policies also play a crucial role in maintaining cloud identity resilience. Clear policies around onboarding, offboarding, and role assignment help ensure that users are granted appropriate permissions from the outset and that access is promptly revoked when no longer needed. Governance frameworks that incorporate approval workflows, logging, and auditing capabilities provide a consistent and transparent approach to managing identities. These policies not only enhance security but also support compliance with industry regulations and internal standards.

Disaster recovery and incident response planning are equally important for identity resilience. Organizations should develop comprehensive response plans that outline the steps to take in the event of an IAM service disruption or a security breach. These plans should include procedures for quickly restoring authentication services, re-establishing critical roles and permissions, and communicating with stakeholders. Regularly testing and updating these plans ensures that teams are prepared to act decisively when an incident occurs. Including identity-specific scenarios in disaster recovery exercises helps identify gaps in coverage and confirms that backup systems, policies, and processes work as intended.

Lastly, staying informed about emerging threats and evolving best practices is critical for maintaining resilience. The identity landscape is constantly changing as attackers develop new techniques and as organizations adopt new technologies. Participating in industry forums, attending security conferences, and following trusted security advisories helps security teams stay ahead of potential risks. By remaining vigilant and proactive, organizations can continuously improve their cloud identity resilience and ensure that their IAM infrastructure remains reliable, secure, and responsive to future challenges.

Cost Optimization for Identity Management Solutions

Managing costs in identity and access management (IAM) solutions is a critical concern for organizations striving to maintain strong security without overextending their budgets. While IAM is a necessary investment to protect user accounts, enforce compliance, and streamline access, it can become a significant financial burden if not carefully planned and maintained. By employing a range of cost optimization strategies, organizations can ensure that their identity management solutions remain efficient, scalable, and cost-effective.

One of the most impactful ways to optimize costs is by selecting the right licensing and subscription models. Many IAM solutions offer tiered pricing structures, allowing organizations to pay only for the features they need. Carefully evaluating these tiers and understanding the organization's actual requirements helps avoid unnecessary spending on advanced capabilities that may not be fully utilized. For instance, a company that primarily needs single sign-on (SSO) and basic role-based access control (RBAC) might choose a lower-tier plan rather than a more expensive enterprise package with advanced analytics and governance features. By aligning licensing choices with actual use cases, organizations can significantly reduce ongoing costs.

Leveraging economies of scale is another effective cost-saving approach. For larger organizations or those undergoing rapid growth, consolidating IAM solutions across multiple business units or regions can lead to lower per-user costs. Rather than deploying separate IAM instances for each subsidiary, a centralized, unified identity platform can serve the entire organization. This approach not only reduces licensing fees but also simplifies administration, maintenance, and support, further driving down costs. Additionally, consolidating IAM solutions often improves negotiating power with vendors, enabling organizations to secure more favorable pricing terms.

Cloud-based IAM solutions often present cost advantages over on-premises deployments. By shifting to a cloud-native identity platform, organizations can reduce capital expenditures on hardware, as well as ongoing maintenance and support costs. Cloud IAM providers handle software updates, patching, and infrastructure management, freeing up internal IT resources and reducing overhead. Moreover, cloud solutions typically offer flexible pricing based on active users, allowing organizations to scale costs in line with their actual usage rather than maintaining excess capacity. This pay-as-you-go model helps organizations avoid the upfront investment and long-term operational costs associated with traditional on-premises IAM systems.

Reducing the complexity of IAM implementations also contributes to cost optimization. Complex environments with numerous overlapping roles, groups, and policies require more administrative effort and often lead to inefficiencies. Simplifying role structures, consolidating redundant permissions, and standardizing access policies can significantly reduce the time and effort required to manage identities. With fewer roles and streamlined workflows, organizations spend less on administrative labor, training, and troubleshooting. Over time, this reduction in complexity translates into measurable cost savings.

Automation is another key factor in lowering IAM costs. By automating routine tasks such as user provisioning, deprovisioning, and password resets, organizations can reduce the reliance on manual processes that consume IT resources. Automated workflows ensure that new employees are granted appropriate access on their first day, that departing employees have their access promptly revoked, and that password changes are handled without involving the help desk. By minimizing manual intervention, organizations save on labor costs, decrease the likelihood of human error, and improve overall efficiency.

Regularly reviewing and optimizing IAM policies and configurations also helps control costs. Over time, organizations may accumulate unused accounts, overly broad permissions, and outdated policies. Conducting periodic audits and cleaning up these configurations ensures that only active, necessary identities remain in the system. Removing dormant accounts reduces licensing costs, while tightening permissions minimizes the administrative burden of managing excessive access. Regular policy reviews also help maintain compliance and reduce the costs associated with audit preparation and remediation efforts.

Investing in training and education for IAM administrators can lead to long-term cost savings. Well-trained personnel are more efficient at managing IAM platforms, troubleshooting issues, and implementing cost-saving measures. By providing ongoing training, organizations can improve administrator productivity, reduce reliance on external consultants, and ensure that internal teams can effectively manage the IAM environment. Over time, these improvements in efficiency and expertise help lower the total cost of ownership for identity management solutions.

Monitoring and reporting tools are valuable for tracking IAM costs and identifying areas for optimization. Detailed usage reports, cost breakdowns, and trend analyses enable organizations to pinpoint which services or features are driving expenses. For example, if usage data reveals that a particular application is rarely accessed, the organization may choose to deactivate its integration or shift it to a less expensive tier. By continuously monitoring IAM costs and usage patterns, organizations can make data-driven decisions that reduce waste and improve cost efficiency.

Collaboration between IT, finance, and business units is essential for achieving cost optimization. When IT teams work closely with finance departments, they gain a better understanding of budget constraints and cost allocation. Business units can provide insights into which applications and services are most critical, helping IT prioritize investments and avoid unnecessary spending. By fostering communication and alignment among these stakeholders, organizations can ensure that IAM expenditures are carefully managed and that cost-saving opportunities are fully explored.

Cost optimization in IAM is an ongoing process that requires careful planning, regular reviews, and strategic decision-making. By selecting appropriate licensing models, consolidating systems, leveraging cloud-native solutions, reducing complexity, and embracing automation, organizations can achieve a secure and efficient identity environment while keeping costs under control.

Enabling Secure Collaboration Across Teams

In today's fast-paced business environment, collaboration among teams is essential for driving innovation, improving efficiency, and delivering quality outcomes. As organizations increasingly rely on digital tools and cloud-based platforms to facilitate this collaboration, maintaining security while ensuring seamless access to resources is a critical challenge. Enabling secure collaboration across teams requires a thoughtful approach to identity and access management (IAM), carefully defined policies, and the right technologies to safeguard sensitive information without hindering productivity.

A foundational principle of secure collaboration is implementing role-based and attribute-based access control. Rather than granting broad, unrestricted access to all users, these models ensure that individuals can only access the information and applications necessary for their specific roles. For example, a marketing team may need access to customer analytics and campaign management tools, while an engineering team might require access to product designs and source code repositories. By clearly defining and enforcing these boundaries, organizations reduce the risk of unauthorized access, prevent data leaks, and maintain compliance with regulatory requirements.

Multi-factor authentication (MFA) is another essential component of secure collaboration. With MFA in place, team members must verify their identities through multiple factors—such as a password and a one-time code sent to their mobile device—before accessing shared resources. This additional layer of security ensures that even if credentials are compromised, unauthorized users cannot gain entry. MFA is particularly valuable when teams collaborate remotely or across different regions, as it provides consistent protection regardless of where users log in. By standardizing MFA for all collaborative platforms, organizations create a more secure environment without introducing unnecessary complexity.

The use of federated identity solutions further simplifies secure collaboration by enabling single sign-on (SSO) across multiple applications and services. With SSO, team members can access all their required tools—such as project management platforms, cloud storage, and communication apps—using a single set of credentials. This approach not only enhances the user experience by reducing the number of passwords they need to manage but also strengthens security by centralizing authentication. Administrators gain better visibility into user activity and can quickly respond to suspicious behavior, ensuring that collaboration remains safe and efficient.

Effective collaboration also depends on well-defined data classification policies. By categorizing data based on its sensitivity, organizations can apply tailored security measures to different types of information. For instance, confidential financial reports might require more stringent access controls and encryption than general marketing materials. Data classification ensures that teams understand the importance of the information they handle and helps administrators enforce appropriate protections. Combined with identity management tools, these policies create a structured approach to managing risk while supporting efficient collaboration.

Continuous monitoring and real-time analytics are crucial for maintaining secure collaboration environments. Identity governance solutions provide detailed insights into who accessed what resources, when, and from where. These solutions can identify unusual patterns, such as multiple failed login attempts, unexpected file downloads, or access from previously unseen devices. By integrating these monitoring tools into their IAM framework, organizations can detect potential threats early, take immediate corrective actions, and maintain the trust of their teams.

Training and awareness programs further enhance secure collaboration. While technical controls are vital, human behavior often determines the effectiveness of security measures. By educating team members about phishing attacks, secure password practices, and the importance of using sanctioned collaboration tools, organizations build a culture of security awareness. When employees understand the risks and their roles in safeguarding data, they are more likely to follow best practices and report suspicious activity promptly.

Secure collaboration also involves carefully managing third-party access. Teams often work with external partners, contractors, and vendors who require limited access to certain resources. Establishing temporary, tightly controlled access policies for these external collaborators is essential. Instead of granting broad permissions, organizations can use identity federation or just-in-time access provisioning to ensure that third parties only access what is necessary, and only for the duration of the project. These approaches minimize exposure and reduce the risk of external breaches.

Adopting a zero-trust security model can further strengthen collaboration security. In a zero-trust environment, no user or device is trusted by default, even if they are inside the network. Every access request is thoroughly verified based on identity, context, and risk level. For instance, a user accessing sensitive financial data from an unfamiliar location might be prompted for additional authentication or temporarily restricted. Zero trust ensures that all collaborative interactions are continually validated, reducing the likelihood of unauthorized access and data leakage.

Finally, integrating secure collaboration into the overall IAM strategy helps organizations maintain consistency and scalability. By unifying collaboration tools under a single identity management platform, administrators can enforce uniform policies, streamline access provisioning, and maintain a centralized view of all user activity. This holistic approach simplifies administration, improves user experience, and ensures that secure collaboration practices evolve alongside organizational growth and changing technological landscapes.

Secure collaboration across teams requires a combination of robust IAM practices, clear policies, advanced authentication methods, continuous monitoring, and ongoing education. By focusing on these elements, organizations can foster an environment where team members work together safely and productively, regardless of their location or the platforms they use.

Preparing for the Next Generation of Identity Challenges

The evolution of technology and the growing complexity of IT environments have introduced a new wave of identity challenges. As organizations embrace cloud computing, mobile workforces, and interconnected devices, the traditional approaches to identity management are no longer sufficient. Preparing for these emerging challenges requires forward-looking strategies, innovative technologies, and a proactive mindset that anticipates how identities will be used and misused in the years ahead. By adapting to these changes, organizations can stay ahead of evolving threats, maintain regulatory compliance, and ensure that their identity systems remain robust and resilient.

One of the most pressing challenges of the next generation is the sheer scale and diversity of identities. The days when identity management primarily focused on employees are long gone. Modern organizations must manage a vast array of identities, including contractors, customers, partners, application services, APIs, and Internet of Things (IoT) devices. Each of these entities requires secure authentication, well-defined access policies, and continuous monitoring. As the number of identities grows, so does the complexity of managing them. To prepare for this challenge, organizations must invest in identity solutions that can handle millions of identities at scale, support multiple identity types, and provide seamless integration across a diverse ecosystem of applications and devices.

Another critical challenge is maintaining identity integrity in a highly distributed environment. As organizations adopt hybrid and multi-cloud strategies, identities often span multiple platforms and regions. Users may access resources from different countries, devices, and networks, making it difficult to establish a consistent security baseline. To address this, identity management must evolve to provide a unified view of identities across all environments. This involves adopting federated identity models, implementing single sign-on (SSO) across multiple cloud providers, and ensuring that access policies are enforced consistently regardless of where the user is located. Achieving this level of integration and consistency is essential for maintaining security, user experience, and regulatory compliance.

The growing sophistication of identity-based attacks is another area of concern. Cybercriminals are increasingly targeting credentials, exploiting identity federation gaps, and leveraging advanced social engineering techniques to gain unauthorized access. Phishing campaigns, credential stuffing attacks, and supply chain compromises are becoming more common and more difficult to detect. Preparing for these threats requires organizations to move beyond traditional password-based authentication. Multi-factor authentication (MFA), adaptive authentication, and behavioral analytics must become standard components of any identity management strategy. Additionally, identity threat detection and response (ITDR) tools can help identify and mitigate identity-based attacks before they cause significant damage.

Privacy and data protection regulations are also driving the need for more advanced identity solutions. As data privacy laws like GDPR and CCPA evolve, organizations must demonstrate that they have robust identity governance in place. This includes ensuring that access is granted only to those who truly need it, maintaining detailed logs of all identity-related activity, and providing users with greater control over their personal data. Preparing for these requirements involves not only technical solutions but also the establishment of clear policies, regular access reviews, and transparent communication with users. By integrating privacy considerations into their identity strategies, organizations can maintain trust and avoid costly penalties.

The rise of decentralized identity models is another factor that organizations must prepare for. Decentralized identity systems, often based on blockchain or distributed ledger technologies, aim to give users more control over their credentials. In this model, individuals store their identity information in digital wallets and share only the necessary data with service providers. This approach reduces reliance on centralized identity providers, improves privacy, and allows users to maintain control of their own data. While decentralized identity is still an emerging technology, it is likely to play a significant role in the future of identity management. Organizations that start exploring and piloting decentralized identity solutions now will be better positioned to adopt them as they become more mainstream.

Artificial intelligence (AI) and machine learning (ML) are also reshaping identity management. These technologies are enabling more sophisticated anomaly detection, risk scoring, and automated policy recommendations. AI-driven tools can identify subtle changes in user behavior that might indicate a compromised account, adjust access levels in real-time based on risk, and streamline identity governance processes. As these technologies mature, they will play a crucial role in helping organizations adapt to rapidly changing environments and emerging threats. Investing in AI and ML capabilities now will ensure that organizations have the tools they need to address future identity challenges.

Another important consideration is the user experience. As identity systems become more complex, ensuring a seamless and intuitive experience for users will be paramount. Passwordless authentication methods, biometric logins, and streamlined self-service capabilities are increasingly expected by both employees and customers. Providing a frictionless user experience not only improves productivity but also reduces the likelihood that users will resort to insecure workarounds. By prioritizing user-centric design and integrating user experience into their identity strategies, organizations can meet both security and usability goals.

Finally, organizations must build a culture of continuous improvement and adaptability. Preparing for the next generation of identity challenges is not a one-time effort; it requires ongoing investment in education, training, and policy refinement. Security teams must stay informed about emerging threats, evolving technologies, and changing regulatory landscapes. Regular reviews of identity management policies, continuous testing of security controls, and a commitment to adopting new best practices ensure that organizations remain prepared for whatever the future holds.

www.ingramcontent.com/pod-product-compliance
Lightning Source LLC
LaVergne TN
LVHW051242050326
832903LV00028B/2522